L e
SO-AZK-369

Social Studies Alive!®
My School and Family

TCi™

Chief Executive Officer: Bert Bower

Chief Operating Officer: Amy Larson

Director of Product Development: Liz Russell

Managing Editor: Laura Alavosus

Editorial Project Manager: Lara Fox

Project Editor: Beverly Cory

Editorial Associates: Anna Embree and Sarah Sudano

Production Manager: Lynn Sanchez

Design Manager: Jeff Kelly

Graphic Designer: Cheri DeBusk

Photo Edit Manager: Margee Robinson

Photo Editor: Diane Austin

Art Editor: Sarah Wildfang

Audio Manager: Katy Haun

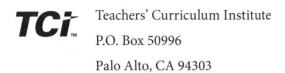

Teachers' Curriculum Institute
P.O. Box 50996
Palo Alto, CA 94303

Customer Service: 800-497-6138

www.teachtci.com

Copyright © 2010 by Teachers' Curriculum Institute.
No parts of the publication may be reproduced without written permission from
the publisher. Printed in the United States of America.

ISBN 978-1-58371-781-3

2 3 4 5 6 7 8 9 10   MLI   15 14 13 12 11 10 09

Program Director

Bert Bower

Program Consultant

Vicki LaBoskey, Ph.D., Professor of Education, Mills College, Oakland, California

Student Edition Writers

Laura M. Alavosus

Abigail Boyce

Susan Buckley

Beverly Cory

Wendy Frey

Curriculum Developers

Joyce Bartky

Nicolle Hutchinson

Reading Specialist

Barbara Schubert, Ph.D., Reading Specialist, Saint Mary's College, Moraga, California

Teacher and Content Consultants

Jill Bartky, Teacher, Sharp Park Elementary School, Pacifica, California

Debra Elsen, Teacher, Manchester Elementary, Manchester, Maryland

Gina Frazzini, Literary Coach, Gatzert Elementary, Seattle, Washington

Patrick J. Lee, Teacher, Ohlone Elementary, Palo Alto, California

Jennifer Miley, Teacher, Duveneck Elementary School, Palo Alto, California

Mitch Pascal, Social Studies Specialist, Arlington County Schools, Arlington, Virginia

Jodi Perraud, Teacher, Boulevard Heights Elementary, Hollywood, Florida

Becky Suthers, Retired Teacher, Stephen F. Austin Elementary, Weatherford, Texas

Literature Consultant

Regina M. Rees, Ph.D., Assistant Professor, Beeghly College of Education, Youngstown State University, Youngstown, Ohio

Music Specialist

Beth Yankee, Teacher, The Woodward School for Technology and Research, Kalamazoo, Michigan

Maps

Mapping Specialists, Ltd. Madison, Wisconsin

Contents

How to Use This Program:
Social Studies Alive! My School and Family

Teaching with the TCI Approach means shifting to a student-centered, activity-based classroom. To meet this exciting challenge, this introduction to the Lesson Guide for *Social Studies Alive! My School and Family* will give you the basics you need to start teaching this program with confidence right away.

The TCI Approach

Why is the TCI Approach so effective at igniting students' passion for learning? The TCI Approach consists of a series of instructional practices that allow students of all abilities to experience key social studies concepts. It has eight important features.

Theory- and Research-Based Active Instruction

Lessons and activities are based on five well-established theories.

Understanding by Design   Grant Wiggins and Jay McTighe maintain that teaching for deep understanding must begin with planning the big ideas students should learn. That's why you will see an Essential Question at the start of every chapter in *Social Studies Alive! My School and Family.*

Nonlinguistic Representation   Research by Robert Marzano and colleagues demonstrates that teaching with nonlinguistic activities helps improve comprehension. Use of movement and graphic note-taking are both key to TCI lessons.

Multiple Intelligences   Howard Gardner believes that all students are intelligent—just not in the same ways. TCI activities address seven of Gardner's intelligences: verbal-linguistic, logical-mathematical, visual-spatial, bodily-kinesthetic, musical-rhythmic, interpersonal, and intrapersonal.

Cooperative Interaction   Elizabeth Cohen's research shows that cooperative groupwork leads to learning gains and higher student achievement. Working in small groups is a cornerstone of TCI activities.

Spiral Curriculum   Jerome Bruner championed the idea of the spiral curriculum, in which students learn progressively—understanding more difficult concepts through a process of step-by-step discovery. TCI questioning strategies spiral from simple recall to higher-order thinking skills such as analysis and evaluation.

Standards-Based Content

Dynamic lessons that integrate hands-on learning and content reading build mastery of state and national standards in both social studies and language arts.

Preview Assignment

Short, engaging exercises at the start of each lesson help you preview key concepts and engage students' knowledge and personal experience. In *Social Studies Alive! My School and Family,* each Preview includes Connecting to Prior Knowledge, Developing Vocabulary, and Building Background Knowledge.

Multiple Intelligences Teaching Strategies

TCI activities incorporate six multiple intelligences teaching strategies:

- Visual Discovery
- Social Studies Skill Builder
- Experiential Exercise
- Writing for Understanding
- Response Group
- Problem Solving Groupwork

These six strategies are explained in detail on the following pages.

Considerate Text

Carefully structured reading materials enable students at all levels to understand what they read. Uncluttered pages present content in digestible "chunks." Engaging images reinforce content, while consistent vocabulary development improves student comprehension.

Graphically Organized Reading Notes

Visually engaging Reading Notes help students record key ideas and make meaning out of what they read. By combining graphic and written work, students improve their comprehension and retention of content.

Processing Assignment

An end-of-lesson assignment involving multiple intelligences and higher-order thinking skills challenges students to apply what they have learned in a variety of creative ways.

Assessments to Inform Instruction

Carefully designed chapter tests move students through a progression of thinking skills, from comprehension to skills application to critical thinking. Test results in these three areas show you where students are succeeding and where they need more instruction.

Multiple Intelligences Teaching Strategies

The TCI Approach uses the six teaching strategies to bring learning alive. All six strategies appear in the *Social Studies Alive! My School and Family* Lesson Guide with detailed, step-by-step instructions. Support materials for each chapter's activities appear in the Lesson Masters, Transparencies, and Placards as well as on the *Sounds of Social Studies* CD and TeachTCI CD-ROM.

Visual Discovery

In Visual Discovery activities, students view, touch, interpret, and bring to life compelling images as they discover key social studies concepts. Seeing and interacting with an image in combination with reading and recording notes helps students remember important content.

Here are some tips for Visual Discovery activities:

- Arrange your classroom so that projected images will be large and clear.
- Ask carefully sequenced questions that lead to discovery.
- Challenge students to read about each image and apply what they learn.
- Have students interact with each image to demonstrate learning.

Social Studies Skill Builder

In Social Studies Skill Builders, students work in pairs or small groups on fast-paced, skill-oriented tasks such as reading maps, categorizing information, analyzing artifacts and primary sources, and comparing and contrasting ideas to enhance their understanding of chapter content.

Here are some tips for Social Studies Skill Builders:

- Teach each skill through modeling and guided practice.
- Prepare students to work in pairs or small groups.
- Set clear expectations, allow students to practice each skill repeatedly, and give immediate feedback.
- Debrief the activity to help students make connections to key concepts.

Experiential Exercise

In Experiential Exercises, participating in short, memorable experiences helps students grasp social studies concepts. Through the use of movement and introspection, students capture a moment or feeling that is central to understanding a particular concept or historical event.

Here are some tips for Experiential Exercises:

- Prepare students for a safe, successful experience by arranging the classroom appropriately, communicating clear behavioral and learning expectations, giving clear directions, anticipating student reactions, and recognizing teachable moments.

- Bring authenticity to the experience by assuming an appropriate persona, hamming it up, and using simple props, costumes, music, and sound effects.
- Allow students to express their feelings immediately after the experience.
- Ask carefully sequenced questions to help students make connections between their experience and key concepts or events.

Writing for Understanding

Writing for Understanding activities begin with a rich experience—such as viewing powerful images, role-playing, discussing complex issues, or acting out key events—to write about. Students develop ideas and form opinions during the experience, before starting to write. The experience becomes a springboard for writing, challenging students to clarify ideas, organize information, and express what they have learned.

Here are some tips for Writing for Understanding activities:

- Have students record their ideas, thoughts, and feelings in prewriting activities.
- Guide students through the writing process.
- Use peer feedback groups as part of the revision process.

Response Group

In Response Group activities, students work in small groups with thought-provoking resources to discuss critical thinking questions among themselves. A presenter then shares each group's findings with the class.

Here are some tips for Response Group activities:

- Create mixed-ability groups and a suitable classroom arrangement.
- Prepare students to answer provocative critical thinking questions.
- Allow groups time to prepare their responses.
- Facilitate a lively class discussion.

Problem Solving Groupwork

In Problem Solving Groupwork activities, students work in heterogeneous groups to create projects that require multiple abilities so that every student can contribute. Within a group, each student takes a defined role. After completing their task, groups present their projects to the class.

Here are some tips for Problem Solving Groupwork activities:

- Review ground rules for working cooperatively in groups.
- Give group members clearly defined roles and requirements.
- Give groups autonomy and time to prepare high-quality projects.
- Allow groups to showcase their work.

Program Components

The components of *Social Studies Alive! My School and Family* work together to maximize your time and creativity. Everything you need to provide insightful and stimulating classroom experiences is included in the program. There are also plenty of opportunities to add your own resources.

Student Edition

For flexible use with beginning readers, the Student Edition comes in both the standard and Big Book formats. Each chapter title poses an Essential Question to help students focus their learning on key concepts. In the Student Edition you will find

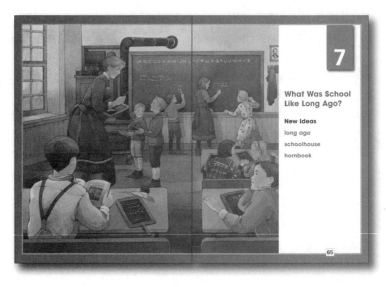

- 14 chapters that introduce basic social studies concepts such as "How do we get along in school?", "What do families need and want?", and "What is a map?"

- considerate text that is uncluttered and easy to navigate.

- graphic elements that spark student interest and foster comprehension.

- highlighted social studies vocabulary terms.

- a high-interest Reading Further case study at the end of each chapter that explores dimensions of the chapter's concepts in depth.

Lesson Guide

"Command Central" for the program, with detailed, step-by-step instructions for each chapter, as well as the following resources to help you plan your lesson:

- a materials list and estimated timing

- both social studies and language arts objectives

- a planning guide for pacing the lesson

- language arts sidebars at point of use to help integrate vocabulary development, reading strategies, writing tips, and speaking and listening into social studies instruction

- suggestions for differentiating instruction for English language learners, students with special needs, and enrichment

- a Guide to Reading Notes and a Guide to Reading Further—answers to objective questions that appear in the Interactive Student Notebook

- suggestions for enhancing learning with online resources and literature connections

- answers for assessments

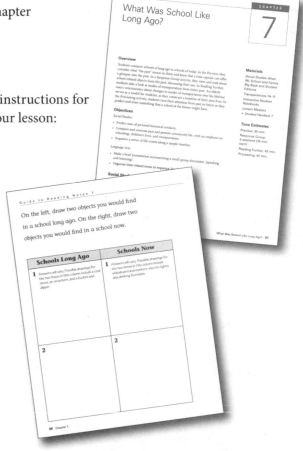

Lesson Masters

Reproducible pages for classroom support, identified in the materials list for each chapter in the Lesson Guide. Includes Student Handouts, Information Masters, and chapter assessments.

Interactive Student Notebook

Each student's personal repository of learning, all in one place. For each chapter, the Interactive Student Notebook includes

- a Preview assignment
- graphically organized Reading Notes
- activity pages to support the Reading Further selection
- a Processing assignment

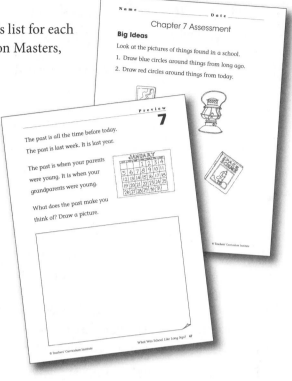

Transparencies and Placards

Visual support for chapter activities, including maps, photographs, and illustrations.

Sounds of Social Studies CD

Audio tracks of songs, dramatizations, and sound effects that play an essential role in several lessons.

Solutions for Effective Instruction

A rich collection of classroom-tested strategies for enriching your teaching through

- integrating reading/language arts
- differentiating instruction
- building social studies/critical thinking skills

Interactive Desk Map

Durable two-sided map to help students improve their geographic knowledge and skills. The Lesson Guide provides specific suggestions for using each map.

TeachTCI

The "home base" for TCI lessons—everything you need for planning and instruction. Includes a CD-ROM with a link to exclusive resources at www.teachtci.com. TeachTCI gives you

- all the materials in the Teacher Resources kit in digital format
- Assessment Creator
- Enrichment Resources
- lesson tips from the TCI community
- customized state correlations

Walking Through a Lesson

While students look forward to the wide variety of activities they will experience in a TCI classroom, they also reap the benefits of TCI's consistent organization of learning in the chapters. Following sound pedagogical practices, each lesson begins with a Preview assignment to spark interest and connect to prior knowledge, progresses through a dynamic class activity and visually engaging Reading Notes, then moves to Reading Further, and concludes with a Processing assignment that asks students to apply what they have learned.

Preview

The Preview assignment is a short, engaging task that foreshadows upcoming content. The goal is to ignite interest, activate prior knowledge, tap a wide range of intelligences, and prepare students to tackle new concepts. The Preview is built around three essentials for frontloading a lesson: Connecting to Prior Knowledge, Developing Vocabulary, and Building Background Knowledge. In *Social Studies Alive! My School and Family*, students take part in activities such as interviewing each other and playing games in the first part of the Preview. Then they complete the Preview assignment in their Interactive Student Notebooks.

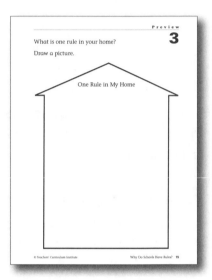

Types of Preview assignments include

- comparing personal experience with key concepts
- predicting
- responding to images
- using interview checklists
- completing word webs

Classroom Activity

At the heart of each TCI lesson is the classroom activity that engages students in social studies content and concepts through hands-on learning experiences. These core activities use the six TCI teaching strategies.

Examples of classroom activities in *Social Studies Alive! My School and Family* include

- Visual Discovery: Who Helps at Us School?
- Social Studies Skill Builder: Why Is It Important to Learn from Each Other?
- Experiential Exercise: Why Do Schools Have Rules?
- Writing for Understanding: How Are Families Special?
- Response Group: What Was School Like Long Ago?
- Problem Solving Groupwork: What Do Families Need and Want?

Reading Notes

One of the most powerful ways to improve students' comprehension and retention is to have them complete graphic Reading Notes for each chapter. When students record information in engaging, visual ways, they are better able to recall social studies content months, and even years, later. Students complete the Reading Notes in their Interactive Student Notebooks.

Types of Reading Notes include

- matrices
- annotated images
- annotated maps
- illustrated riddles
- game grids

Reading Further

To support the Reading Further in every chapter of the Student Edition, students complete a page in their Interactive Student Notebooks.

Types of Reading Further activities include

- finishing dialogues
- reading maps
- creating illustrated timelines
- retelling stories in sequence
- drawing environmental and travel posters
- identifying problems and solutions

Processing

Processing assignments are wrap-up activities that challenge students to synthesize the information in a chapter to demonstrate their understanding. The intent is to allow students to apply what they have learned actively so that you—and they—can assess their comprehension. Students encounter the Processing assignment in their Interactive Student Notebooks.

Types of Processing assignments include

- predictive drawings
- illustrated personal reflections
- sensory-detail pages for a class book
- classroom maps
- captioned illustrations
- service awards
- action plans
- labeled squares for a class quilt

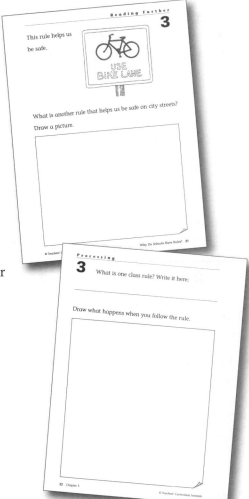

Organizing a TCI Classroom

Most of the *Social Studies Alive! My School and Family* activities require students to move into small groups of two, three, or four. With a brief training exercise, you can teach students how to form groups quickly without wasting valuable time.

Moving Your Classroom Furniture

Tell students that they will be working in small groups of different sizes throughout the year. They must know how to move into each grouping quickly and efficiently, with all their materials. When working in pairs, they should place their desks either side by side or face to face, with the edges touching. For groups of three or more, the front corners of the desks must touch.

With these expectations clear, allow students to practice moving into groups. Randomly assign students to groups and indicate where they should meet. Then say "Go!" and time them. If necessary, allow the class to discuss what went wrong and brainstorm ideas for getting into groups more efficiently. Have students repeat the process until they can do it in "record time."

If you spend time at the beginning of the school year teaching this skill, you will save hours of instructional time. Your goal should be for students to be able to form various group configurations in less than one minute, without your needing to touch any student furniture.

Organizing Your Teacher Resources

Social Studies Alive! My School and Family comes with all the materials you need to excite your students. It will be up to you, however, to gather the materials for each chapter and organize them in a way that makes it fast and easy to conduct activities year after year. Here are some tips to save you time and make running your classroom much easier:

- Begin preparation for each activity by gathering everything on the materials list, such as Placards, Transparencies, and the *Sounds of Social Studies* CD. Consider opening the Lesson Guide and Lesson Masters on the appropriate TeachTCI CD-ROM and printing out all pages of both.

- Make all the copies you will need of Lesson Masters, such as assessments, Student Handouts, and Information Masters.

- When you finish each activity, place all the printed materials in a clear, resealable plastic bag (an ideal size is 10 by 12 inches) with the Lesson Guide on top as a "label." This will keep the many individual activity pieces together and will ensure that next year's preparation takes virtually no time.

Creating a Cooperative, Tolerant Classroom

The interactive, experiential, and stimulating learning at the heart of the TCI Approach can happen only when students feel comfortable sharing ideas, taking risks, working cooperatively, tolerating differences, and disagreeing honestly and respectfully with you and their classmates. Thus, you need to take purposeful steps to develop a "safe" community in your classroom.

Here are some tips for creating a cooperative, tolerant classroom:

- Greet your students at the door every day to make a personal connection with them as they enter your classroom.
- Explain your expectations for classroom behavior, using specific examples. You may also involve students in shaping class rules.
- Convince students that learning to work effectively with others will benefit them throughout their lives.
- Teach students how to move efficiently into groups of various sizes.
- Use role-playing activities to teach students cooperative skills.
- Form mixed-ability groups.

You may wish to make a poster of these reminders for your classroom:

How to Work Cooperatively in Groups

1. Smile, be friendly, and introduce yourself.
2. Sit properly.
3. Look at the person talking.
4. Listen.
5. Take turns.
6. Be helpful and nice.
7. Work out problems on your own.
8. Follow directions and stay on task.

Using the Interactive Student Notebook

In the Interactive Student Notebook, all parts of the integrated lesson come together as students create a dynamic record of their learning. Unlike traditional worksheets, the activities in the notebook reach out to students, inviting them to be active participants in their own learning. The notebook encourages students to use a variety of intelligences, not just linguistic intelligence. Especially important for the primary grades, the notebook helps students to organize systematically as they learn. Over the course of the school year, the notebook becomes a portfolio of individual learning. Teachers, students, and even family members can review a student's progress in writing, thinking, and organization skills. This makes the notebook a valuable tool for parent conferences.

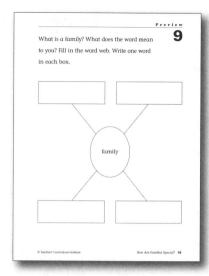

Interactive Student Notebook Guidelines for Students

Teachers use the Interactive Student Notebook in a variety of forms. Some give their students the consumable notebook that is provided with TCI's core program materials. Teachers who elect to use this consumable can follow the sequence exactly as designed, having students complete the specified Previews, Reading Notes, Reading Furthers, and Processing assignments. This system is helpful to teachers who are new to the TCI Approach, since they can rely on the published Interactive Student Notebook for support while they are learning to use the essential elements and strategies of the program.

Other teachers elect to supplement the printed notebook with their own handouts and materials that students bring to school. You will notice that the Interactive Student Notebook is punched and perforated to give you flexibility in how you use it. You may wish to have students use spiral-bound notebooks, clasp folders, or three-ring binders to combine the materials, cutting and pasting as they create their own unique Interactive Student Notebooks. In this format, the TCI materials serve as the backbone, but teachers have the flexibility to tailor instruction to suit their needs.

Regardless of the format you plan to use, the following hints will increase the effectiveness of your Interactive Student Notebooks and allow students' individual styles to flourish.

- Supply materials that inspire creativity. An abundance of materials—colored pencils and markers, scissors, glue sticks, colored highlighters—will spark creativity for notebook assignments.

- Let students create their own covers. Encourage students to create a colorful cover that reflects what they are learning. This immediately sends the message that the notebooks will be their own creations that they can take pride in, and it helps cut down on the number of lost notebooks during the year.

- Personalize the notebooks with an author page. Have each student create a page about himself or herself to include at the front of the notebook. With both a personalized cover and an author page, very few notebooks will get lost.

- Establish clear guidelines for student work. Decide ahead of time what you expect your students to produce in their notebooks, and clearly communicate your expectations. It will be helpful to model neatness and accuracy for students, particularly in the beginning of the year.

Managing Assessment of Interactive Student Notebooks

Because so much of students' work appears in these notebooks, you will need an efficient and accurate system for assessing them.

Informal Assessment   Monitor student notebooks aggressively in the first few weeks of school. Look at notebooks as you walk around, making positive comments and helpful suggestions. Here are some additional ideas:

- While students work on another assignment, conduct a quick review of previous work, giving students checks or special stamps to denote completed assignments.
- Provide a model of outstanding work for an assignment or set of class notes.
- Allow students to use their notebooks on a quiz or test. This will come as a pleasant surprise and reward for students with well-organized notebooks.

Formal Assessment   At the beginning of the year, clearly explain the criteria on which you will evaluate notebooks, such as quality and completeness of assignments, visual appearance, neatness, higher-order thinking, and organization. Here are some additional ideas for assessing student work:

- Create a simple rubric that identifies the criteria you feel are most important. Post it in your classroom.
- Stagger notebook collection so that you correct only one portion of the class at a time.
- Grade selectively. Don't feel compelled to grade every notebook entry.
- Have students assess their own work. This process enables them to reflect on their learning and critically review their progress. Explain that if your assessment differs markedly from theirs—better or worse—they will have the opportunity to discuss the reasons for your assessment.

Integrating Reading and Language Arts

In recent years, many elementary teachers have found it harder and harder to find time for social studies. With greater emphasis on reading instruction, writing, and math, there seems to be less time to fit in any history or geography, civics, or economics. Yet these subjects are essential to the development of young minds and of responsible citizens in our democracy.

Social Studies Alive! My School and Family makes it easy for you to bring social studies back into your curriculum. With many features to help you reinforce what you are already teaching in reading and language arts, you can "multitask" as you teach social studies. Here's how:

Vocabulary Development

Studies have shown that vocabulary is the single strongest predictor of successful student comprehension. For this reason, key social studies terms get special treatment, identified in bold, blue type on the opening page of each chapter of the Student Edition.

To help you teach these terms, the overview page for each chapter in the Lesson Guide alerts you to new vocabulary. Each Preview section in the Lesson Guide indicates when to introduce and reteach the terms. Throughout the Procedures section in the Lesson Guide, tinted sidebars at point of use suggest more ways to amplify vocabulary development. And in *Solutions for Effective Instruction*, you will find many other techniques for helping your students master new words.

High-interest Content and Reading Strategies

What better way to create lifelong readers than to introduce primary students to exciting and interesting text? Every chapter in the Student Edition of *Social Studies Alive! My School and Family* has two types of reading. The first part of the chapter presents essential concepts with considerate language and pictures that young students can relate to. The second part of the chapter is an engaging case study delving deeper into a chapter concept. For example, in Chapter 2, "Why Is It Important to Learn from Each Other?", students read and discuss the fable of the ant and the grasshopper.

The Lesson Guide includes detailed Procedures to help you teach students how to read informational text. It also has tinted sidebars at point of use with suggestions for specific reading strategies to help students master the content.

The Interactive Student Notebook is set up to help students develop a purpose for reading, take memorable notes on what they've read, extend the concept presented in Reading Further, and synthesize what they've learned in creative ways.

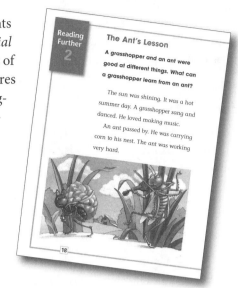

Writing Assignments

Good writing is the expression of good thinking. Stating ideas clearly in writing is a key element of literacy, but it is a skill that takes constant practice to learn. Throughout the Lesson Guide, you will find careful instructions for numerous writing assignments—simple sentences, descriptions, comparisons and contrasts, stories, and personal experiences—that students will complete in their Interactive Student Notebooks in Preview, Reading Notes, Reading Further, and Processing assignments. Each chapter test also includes a prompt for student response. As the year progresses, you will be able to see students progress from simple to more detailed tasks.

Additional writing tips appear in tinted sidebars at point of use in the Lesson Guide and in *Solutions for Effective Instruction*.

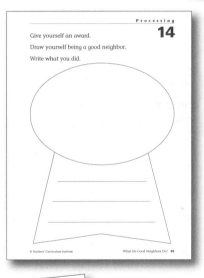

Additional Reading Opportunities

A love of reading comes from frequent exposure to great books. To supplement *Social Studies Alive! My School and Family*, each chapter in the Lesson Guide includes an annotated list of books that extend and enrich the content of the lesson. The annotated list appears on the Enhancing Learning page. Some of these books are for you to read to students, and others are books that students can read themselves.

Assessing Learning

Effective assessment requires many approaches—individual and group, informal and formal—to create a well-rounded understanding of student performance. Here are some tips for evaluating student work.

Informal Assessment

Assessment of day-to-day activities benefits both you and your students. You send the message that every activity is important. And by identifying what works and what doesn't, you are able to adjust your instructional plans. Try these methods:

- Make your expectations known in advance so students will know how they will be rated.
- Note a student's answers to questions, both oral and written.
- Evaluate participation in act-it-outs and class discussions.
- Look for a student's level of cooperation in a pair or small group.
- Ask students to assess their own work.
- Skim notebooks as students work in class.

Groupwork Assessment

Evaluating groupwork presents a lot of questions: Should you rate the product or the process? The individual or the group? The amount of effort or the quality of the result? Here are five steps that will help you assess groupwork equitably:

1. Set clear criteria for evaluation.
2. Make both individuals and groups accountable.
3. Record notes as groups work and while they present their final products.
4. Have students complete self-assessments to evaluate their individual contributions as well as the group's performance.
5. Determine group and individual grades.

Formal Assessment

In addition to classroom observations and evaluation of student notebooks, you will need formal measurements of how much your students have learned. Research has shown that the TCI Approach improves student comprehension and retention. (For research results, visit www.teachtci.com.) *Social Studies Alive! My School and Family* provides assessment at the end of each chapter. You will find reproducible test pages in the Lesson Masters and answers in the Lesson Guide.

Each chapter assessment has two parts. The first part, "Big Ideas," consists of multiple-choice and matching questions. Students will find it helpful to review their Reading Notes in their Interactive Student Notebooks as preparation for these questions. One question about the Reading Further selection is included.

In the second part, "Show You Know," students must use higher-order thinking skills to respond to drawing and writing prompts. These open-response questions are scaffolded to help students understand what to do.

You will find digital versions of the assessments on the TeachTCI CD-ROM, both in PDF format and in the Assessment Creator. With the Assessment Creator, you can use each test as is, randomize the order of questions, edit questions, or add your own questions.

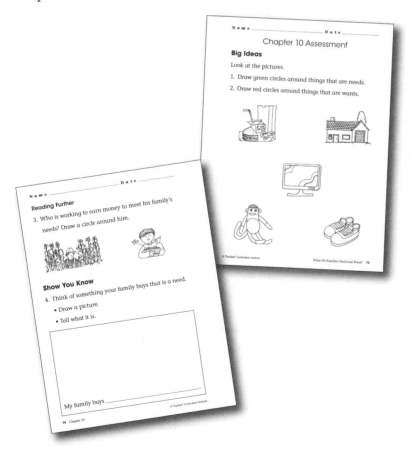

Enhancing Instruction with TeachTCI

Support for *Social Studies Alive! My School and Family* extends beyond the box of print and audiovisual materials to a wealth of technology components. With the TeachTCI CD-ROM and a code that provides access to exclusive online resources, you will have the following tools to help with planning and extending the lessons and customizing your assessment.

All the Materials in the Teacher Resources Kit, in Digital Format

Access digital versions of components, such as the Lesson Guide, Lesson Masters, Interactive Student Notebook, *Sounds of Social Studies* CD, Transparencies, and Placards. All materials are organized by chapter. Preview and print items as needed.

Assessment Creator

Build customized assessments for your class. This tool lets you add, delete, edit, and sort questions and answers.

Lesson Tips from the TCI Community

Get ideas for your own classroom, engage in professional exchanges with teachers around the country, and share your own best practices. Our discussion groups are now organized by program and chapter.

Enrichment Resources

Enhance student learning with chapter-related Web site links and supplemental readings that further support state standards.

Customized State Correlations

See how the content you are teaching aligns to your state standards in easy-to-read chart form.

Growing Professionally

Creating long-lasting change in today's social studies classroom is hard work. You need new ideas, realistic strategies, and ongoing support.

TCI Academy, the professional development division of TCI, can help make learning come alive for all students at your school or in your district. We offer more than 20 professional development sessions for elementary teachers on topics such as content literacy, teaching American history, differentiating instruction, and many more.

TCI Academy Trainers are classroom teachers with years of experience helping their colleagues become highly successful and effective teachers. Our Trainers will partner with you to ensure your school or district receives the latest training in a highly engaging manner. In addition to on-site training, TCI Academy's on-site consulting is a powerful way for school and districts to improve instruction in social studies. On-site consulting combines direct instruction, classroom observation, and demonstration lessons to help teachers implement TCI's curricular programs and strategies to their full potential.

For a complete listing of TCI Academy sessions, please visit our Web site at www.tciacademy.com or call us at 800-840-2698.

Letter to Families

The model letter on the following page is designed to tell families what topics you will cover with *Social Studies Alive! My School and Family*, how you will teach their children—using the exciting TCI Approach—and the ways you will incorporate language arts instruction into your teaching of social studies. It also includes tips on providing support at home.

Using the Letter to Families

1. *Reproduce the letter.* You may find it more effective to create your own letter based on the model provided. A customized letter might include rules and procedures that are specific to your classroom.

2. *Send the letter home with students during the first week of school.* Open the lines of communication early. The same letter, or another version of it, should also be available for Back to School Night.

3. *Encourage parents to monitor progress throughout the year by reviewing their child's Interactive Student Notebook.* The Interactive Student Notebook will give parents an overview of their child's learning. During parent conferences, you can use the Interactive Student Notebook to demonstrate where students are excelling and where they are struggling. You may want to have parents sign the Interactive Student Notebook each week to ensure that they are continually monitoring their child's progress.

Dear Families,

This year will be an exciting one for the students in my class. They will be learning key social studies concepts in a highly engaging way.

Our class is using *Social Studies Alive! My School and Family*, a program that truly engages students in learning. Your child will be an active participant, experiencing social studies through innovative teaching practices that include dramatic role-playing, creative simulations, dynamic group projects, and writing activities.

Curious about what your child will be learning this year? First grade is a time of giant steps in learning—not only the three Rs, but social learning as well. Some of the topics we will cover in social studies include *How do we get along in school? Why is it important to learn from each other? Why do schools have rules? How are families special? What do families need and want? How do family members care for each other? What are family traditions? What do good neighbors do?*

As the class works on social studies, I will be giving students many opportunities to practice what they are learning in reading and language arts. Your child will have an Interactive Student Notebook on which to write, draw, and answer questions. Follow your child's work throughout the year and you will see progress not only in social studies knowledge but also in communication skills.

Here are some tips for supporting your child's academic progress in this class:

- Discuss social studies and current events with your child, and listen to what your child has to say.
- Ask to see the Interactive Student Notebook on a regular basis so you can see for yourself what your child is learning.
- Provide a quiet study place, free from distractions.
- Finally, extend learning beyond the walls of the classroom. Take your child to historical sites or museums, to local government buildings or events where you can experience civics in action, and to outdoor places or other sites that support your child's study of geography. Point out that social studies is all around us, that it shapes the present and the future and the way we live, and that every one of us can play an active and positive role in it.

Thank you in advance for your support. I am looking forward to an exciting, enjoyable, and enriching year working with you and your child.

Sincerely,

Your child's teacher

How Do We Get Along in School?

Overview

Students learn about their responsibilities as classmates while they explore ways to get along in school. In the Preview, they consider how cooperation would have helped two stubborn goats. In an Experiential Exercise, they work together to draw a picture and discover the value of cooperating to complete a task. In Reading Further, students learn how some neighbors in New York City cooperated to save a community garden. In the Processing activity, they illustrate another example of how they get along in school, especially when conflicts arise.

Objectives

Social Studies

- Predict outcomes of behavior.
- Identify students' responsibilities to one another in the school community.
- Identify the benefits of cooperating in school.
- Name four ways of cooperating in school.
- Describe the results of one neighborhood's efforts at cooperation.

Language Arts

- Share ideas and plans with a partner. (speaking and listening)
- Read song lyrics as a shared reading experience. (reading)
- Write a short sentence from a model. (writing)

Social Studies Vocabulary

share, talk, listen, take turns

Materials

Social Studies Alive! My School and Family
Big Book and Student Editions

Transparencies 1A and 1B

Interactive Student Notebooks

Lesson Masters
- Information Masters 1A and 1B

CD Track 1

Time Estimates

Preview: 20 min.

Experiential Exercise:
2 sessions (30 min. each)

Reading Further: 35 min.

Processing: 30 min.

Activity	Suggested Time	Materials
Preview • Building Background Knowledge • Developing Vocabulary	20 minutes	• Interactive Student Notebooks • Information Master 1A
Experiential Exercise Identifying the reasons for and types of cooperative behavior	*Phase 1* 30 minutes • The benefits of cooperation (Steps 1–4) *Phase 2* 30 minutes • Four types of cooperative behavior (Steps 5–8)	• drawing paper and crayon (1 each per pair) • *Social Studies Alive! My School and Family* Big Book and Student Editions, Sections 1.1–1.4 • Transparency 1A • Interactive Student Notebooks • Information Master 1B (1 transparency, optional) • CD Track 1
Reading Further Learning about how one neighborhood cooperated to save a community garden	35 minutes	• *Social Studies Alive! My School and Family* Big Book, Chapter 1 Reading Further • Transparency 1B • Interactive Student Notebooks
Processing Drawing and describing an example of cooperative behavior	30 minutes	• *Social Studies Alive! My School and Family* Student Editions, Chapter 1 Summary • Interactive Student Notebooks • CD Track 1
Assessment	15 minutes	• Chapter 1 Assessment, Lesson Masters • Chapter 1 Assessment, Digital Teacher Resources

Preview

1 **Building Background Knowledge:** Read aloud the short folk tale found on *Information Master 1A: Two Goats on a Bridge,* stopping midway through.

- Ask: *What's happening in this story? What is the problem?*

- Have students turn to Preview 1 in their Interactive Student Notebooks. Ask them to draw a picture that shows what they think will happen next in the story.

- Call on volunteers to share their ideas with the class. Then read the rest of the story.

- Lead a discussion of the tale based on questions like these: *How did the two goats try to solve their problem? Did their way work? Why or why not? What are some other ways the goats might have tried to solve their problem?*

- Introduce the term *cooperation.* Explain that *cooperation* is a word that we use to mean "working together and getting along together in a way that is fair for everyone." Ask: *Did the goats cooperate with each other? How could they have cooperated in a way that was fair to both of them?*

2 **Developing Vocabulary:** Cover New Ideas—*share, talk, listen,* and *take turns*—as they arise in the text. You may want to discuss some terms before beginning the activity, using methods described in *Solutions for Effective Instruction.*

Information Master 1A

Experiential Exercise

Phase 1: Identifying the Benefits of Cooperation

1 **Introduce the game *Two on a Task.***

- Tell students they are going to play a drawing game. Group them in pairs. Give one crayon and one sheet of drawing paper to each pair.

- Explain the rules of the game:

  1. Work together with your partner to draw a picture.

  2. Use the same crayon at the same time. Both of you must keep one hand on the crayon at all times.

  3. Work in silence. No talking during the game.

- Before pairs begin to draw, have them close their eyes and imagine the picture they want to draw. Remind students that they may not talk or share their ideas. They must keep their picture ideas to themselves.

- Give pairs two to three minutes to draw. As they work, note their reactions to share during the debriefing.

2 Debrief this first round of the game to help students identify the difficulties of working together without cooperating. Ask such questions as:

- How did you feel trying to draw this way? *(clumsy, funny, couldn't do it)*

- Were you able to draw the picture you imagined?

- What made this task hard? *(two people trying to guide the crayon, couldn't talk to share ideas)*

- Was this the best way to complete a drawing? What could we do to make this drawing activity easier? *(take turns guiding the crayon, talk to each other, share ideas about what to make)*

3 Conduct a second round of *Two on a Task*. Distribute another sheet of drawing paper to each pair. Explain that one game rule changes: this time, partners may talk to each other. Remind them of the other two rules, which do not change: they work together on the same drawing, and both partners must still keep one hand on the crayon at all times. Give pairs another two to three minutes to draw.

4 Debrief the second round to help students identify the benefits of cooperating. Ask such questions as:

- How did you feel this time? *(better, more comfortable)*

- How did your picture turn out? *(better, closer to what I imagined)*

- Why do you think you had a better experience the second time? *(because we took turns guiding the crayon, because we could talk, because we shared ideas)*

- What did you learn about cooperating during this activity?

Explain that cooperating is one of their responsibilities as students in your classroom. Be sure they understand that a responsibility is the same as a duty—something you are supposed to do.

Phase 2: Describing Four Types of Cooperative Behavior

5 Introduce the chapter. Use the *Social Studies Alive! My School and Family* Big Book or project *Transparency 1A: How Do We Get Along in School?* to introduce the New Ideas: *share, talk, listen, take turns.* Discuss the opening illustration. Ask such questions as:

- What details do you see?

- What place is this?

- What do you see children sharing?

- Which children are cooperating?

6 Read aloud Sections 1.1–1.4 from the Big Book. Have students briefly discuss the questions posed. Ask them to describe what the children in the pictures are doing to cooperate and to get along with one another. Help them recognize sharing, talking, listening, and taking turns as ways to head off conflict, which is one of each student's personal responsibilities at school.

Vocabulary Development: Develop Concepts

Create a three-column chart titled "Cooperate." Write these column headings: "Looks like," "Sounds like," and "Feels like." Ask students for observations about their experiences in which classmates cooperated. Add words to the chart as their understanding of the concept increases.

Transparency 1A

7 Play CD Track 1, "The Getting Along Song."

- Help students learn the lyrics by listening and singing along. You may want to make a transparency of *Information Master 1B: The Getting Along Song* and display these lyrics during the song.

- Point out that all the ways of getting along that are mentioned in the song are things we can do to cooperate with one another in school and at home. Review the term *cooperation* and discuss its importance for life at school.

8 Focus on the four cooperative behaviors discussed in the text as students complete Reading Notes 1.

- Read aloud Section 1.1 in *Social Studies Alive! My School and Family* as students follow along. Ask for volunteers to answer this question: *What do we share?*

- Have students turn to Reading Notes 1 in their Interactive Student Notebooks. Read aloud and explain the directions. Model using crayons of different colors, and have students color in each crayon on the page as a reminder of which color to use for each part. Have them use a red crayon to circle two pictures for "we share." They may find more than two examples in the picture. Have them explain their choices.

- Continue reading the Student Edition together, looking at Sections 1.2–1.4 one at a time. Point out that talking, listening, and taking turns in school are their responsibilities as classmates. Ask about ways of being fair when they do these things. Explore the importance of being honest and truthful when talking and listening, so that everyone truly understands one another. Have students use blue, green, and purple crayons as they complete Reading Notes 1, circling two examples each of talking, listening, and taking turns.

Information Master 1B

> **Reading Tip:**
> **Do Shared Reading**
>
> Present the lyrics to "The Getting Along Song" on the transparency or on a large chart for shared reading. Highlight the words *get along, share, talk, listen,* and *take turns.* Use a pointer to track the words as students listen to the CD. Then have students join you in reading the lyrics, with and without the song playing.

Reading Further: A Place to Share

1 Project *Transparency 1B: A Place to Share.* Ask the following visual discovery questions to help students make some predictions.

- What do you see in this picture?

- Where do you think this is?

- What do you think the woman might be planning to do? What makes you think so?

- If we wanted to change this trash-filled lot in some way, to make it prettier or more useful, what could we do?

- How could we cooperate as a group to do that?

2 Open the Big Book to Reading Further 1. Explain that in this story, someone turns this vacant lot into a garden—but then there is a problem. Neighbors work together as a group to solve the problem. Help the class brainstorm the advantages to working in groups to solve problems (easier, faster, more ideas, more fun, and so on).

Transparency 1B

3 **Read pages 8–11 of the Big Book aloud as students follow along.** After reading, review the story with questions such as these:

- When Mrs. Foster saw the lot full of trash, what did she decide to do with it?

- What do you think she and her children did with the trash they picked up? Could they have recycled any of it?

- Did the other people in the neighborhood like what Mrs. Foster did? Why or why not?

- What did the city do to the gate to Mrs. Foster's garden?

- If the city sold the lot, what do you think would happen to the garden? What could someone put on the lot instead?

- After the city said that they wanted to sell the garden lot, the people in the neighborhood had to decide what to do. What were their two choices?

- The people had the right to make either choice. Why do you think they made the choice they did? What made so many of them go to the city to speak up for keeping the garden?

- What are some of the ways this garden is good for the neighborhood?

- "Mo' Pals" is another way of saying "More Friends." Why do you think this city neighborhood chose that name for their garden?

4 **Have students open their Interactive Student Notebooks to Reading Further 1 and consider the vacant lot pictured there.** Tell the students to imagine that this is a small bit of land that their class can fix up in some way. Ask for ideas about what they might do. List these ideas on the board. Possibilities for improved use of the space might include a vegetable garden, a playground with play equipment, a park with trees and flowers, a paved court with basketball hoops, or a skateboard park.

5 **Ask students to support their choice for using the space.** On the board, list their arguments for and against the different choices. As needed, remind them of their responsibility to respect one another's ideas. Then say: *Some of you have different ideas about how to use this space. But the class needs to agree on one way. In making up our minds, we all need to get along. You have talked and listened to one another's ideas. What would be a fair way to decide what to do?* Students might suggest, for example, dividing the lot into different areas or voting to decide on the solution that most people favor.

6 **When the class has agreed on a solution, have students draw their vision for improving the lot.** As a model for students to use in completing the sign over the improved lot, write appropriate words on the board. Ask one or two volunteers to show their work and to review how they cooperated and got along with their classmates in making the final plan for the lot.

Processing

1 **Review four ways to get along in school, cooperate, respect others, and behave responsibly.** Have students sing along with CD Track 1, "The Getting Along Song."

2 **Review the chapter to prepare for Processing 1.** Read aloud the Summary in the Student Edition. Then have students brainstorm other ways to get along in school. Help them think about ways they can cooperate in response to conflicts that often arise in the classroom and on the playground. Write their ideas on the board.

3 **Have students open their Interactive Student Notebooks to Processing 1.** Read the directions aloud. Then tell the students to illustrate one idea from their brainstorming, showing something they can do to get along in school. Help them describe their picture in a sentence. As appropriate, refer them to words you have listed on the board.

> **Writing Tip: Use a Model**
>
> Provide a model based on sentence structures in the Chapter 1 text: "We get along by_____."
>
> Students may use this to label the picture they draw in Processing 1.

Assessment

Masters for the chapter assessment appear in the *Lesson Masters*. Answers appear below.

Big Ideas

1. color blue: children jumping rope

2. color red: children in sandbox

3. Answers will vary. Drawings should reflect an understanding of what makes a garden (e.g., flowers, plants, vegetables).

Show You Know

4. Answers will vary. Drawings should suggest a way of getting along at school.

English Language Learners

Leave the CD with "The Getting Along Song" in a listening center, along with a copy of the lyrics on Information Master 1B. In the lyrics, highlight the new terms *share, talk, listen,* and *take turns.* This will help students become more familiar with the language and the concept of getting along.

Students with Special Needs

For Reading Notes 1 in the Interactive Student Notebook, distribute just one crayon at a time. After students use the red crayon to complete the section for "we share," collect that crayon and distribute a blue crayon for "we talk." Continue in this way with the other colors. Students will be more successful if they have only one crayon at a time.

Enrichment

If there are students who are highly interested in the Reading Further activity, help them find a project to improve the school community while they practice their cooperation skills: sharing, talking, listening, and taking turns. For example, they might cooperate in daily raising and lowering the school flags, sorting recyclable trash, or collecting aluminum cans. Or they could work on a project that improves the community as a whole: collecting food for a food bank or collecting blankets, clothing, and toiletries for a homeless shelter. Have the students share their ideas for a project with the class, listen to one another, talk with partners, and finally vote on a project. Create a chart that shows how the students will take turns working on the project.

Enrichment Resources

Have students find out more about cooperation and getting along by exploring the following Enrichment Resources for *Social Studies Alive! My School and Family* at www.learntci.com.

Internet Connections

These recommended Web sites provide useful and engaging content that enforces skills development and mastery of subjects within the chapter.

Enrichment Readings

These in-depth readings encourage students to explore selected topics related to the chapter. For Chapter 1, you may wish to use one or more of the Enrichment Readings listed for the chapter. You may also find readings that relate the chapter's content directly to your state's curriculum.

Additional Reading Opportunities

These fiction and nonfiction books, which can be read aloud to students, offer opportunities to extend the content in this chapter.

The Garden of Happiness by Erika Tamar. Illustrated by Barbara Lambase. (New York: Harcourt Children's Books, 1996)
In a story similar to that of the Mo' Pals Community Garden, people come together to reclaim a garbage-filled lot. The story is told through the eyes of Marisol, whose own contribution to the garden is an enormous sunflower.

How to Be a Friend by Laurie Krasny Brown. Illustrated by Marc Brown. (New York: Little, Brown, 1998)
This "guide to making and keeping friends" deals with important social issues such as shyness, bullying, ways to be friendly, and conflict resolution.

The Recess Queen by Alexis O'Neill. Illustrated by Laura Huliska-Beith. (New York: Scholastic, 2002)
Mean Jean is the biggest bully on the school playground until a new student in class challenges Jean's right to be the recess queen. This story inspires students to learn to resolve differences and welcome new people into their community.

Answers may vary. Possible answers are shown.

RED

Circle 2 ways we share.

BLUE

Circle 2 ways we talk.

GREEN

Circle 2 ways we listen.

PURPLE

Circle 2 ways we take turns.

take turns (purple)

share (red)

take turns (purple)

listen (green)

talk (blue)

Why Is It Important to Learn from Each Other?

Overview

Students discover the importance of learning from and accepting one another. In the Preview, they use a checklist to explore their similarities and differences. In a Social Studies Skill Builder, students complete questionnaires that reveal their own interests and special talents. They then practice appropriate ways to talk and listen. Reading Further presents an Aesop's fable, in which a carefree grasshopper wishes he had learned from an industrious ant. Finally, in the Processing activity, students color gift boxes to express in code their classmates' unique personalities.

Objectives

Social Studies

- Identify similarities and differences among classmates.
- Compare and contrast classmates' personal preferences and talents.
- Categorize classmates according to their special talents.
- Analyze the costs and benefits of different choices.

Language Arts

- Demonstrate considerate conversational behavior. (speaking and listening)
- Read a fable and identify the moral. (reading)

Social Studies Vocabulary

alike, different, learn

Materials

Social Studies Alive! My School and Family Big Book and Student Editions

Transparencies 2A–2C

Interactive Student Notebooks

Lesson Masters
- Information Master 2
- Student Handouts 2A–2C

CD Track 2

Time Estimates

Preview: 40 min.

Social Studies Skill Builder: 3 sessions (30 min. each)

Reading Further: 30 min.

Processing: 30 min.

Activity	Suggested Time	Materials
Preview • Connecting to Prior Knowledge • Building Background Knowledge • Developing Vocabulary	40 minutes	• *Social Studies Alive! My School and Family* Big Book, Chapter 2 introduction (or Transparency 2A) • Interactive Student Notebooks
Social Studies Skill Builder Comparing and contrasting personal characteristics	*Phase 1* 30 minutes • Identifying individual interests and talents (Steps 1–3) *Phase 2* 30 minutes • Practicing cooperative interaction (Steps 4–9) *Phase 3* 30 minutes • Reviewing the importance of people's similarities and differences (Steps 10–13)	• *Social Studies Alive! My School and Family* Big Book, Sections 2.1–2.4 • Student Handout 2A (1 per student) • Information Master 2 • CD Track 2 • Student Handout 2B (1 per student, trimmed) • *Social Studies Alive! My School and Family* Big Book and Student Editions, Sections 2.1–2.4 • Interactive Student Notebooks • Information Master 2 (1 transparency) • CD Track 2
Reading Further Reading a fable	30 minutes	• *Social Studies Alive! My School and Family* Big Book, Chapter 2 Reading Further • Transparency 2B • Interactive Student Notebooks
Processing Coloring a symbol to represent a unique classmate	30 minutes	• Transparency 2C • Interactive Student Notebooks • Student Handout 2C (1 per student)
Assessment	15 minutes	• Chapter 2 Assessment, Lesson Masters • Chapter 2 Assessment, Digital Teacher Resources

Preview

1 **Connecting to Prior Knowledge:** Have students identify a variety of class-room activities and think about the ones they like best.

Transparency 2A

- Display *Social Studies Alive! My School and Family* Big Book pages 12 and 13 or project *Transparency 2A: Why Is It Important to Learn from Each Other?* Ask: *What do you see? What are the different children doing?*

- After the class briefly identifies what each child or group is doing, ask: *If you could walk into this classroom, which child or group of children would you most like to join? What would you be doing? How is that activity like something you do either in our classroom or at home?*

- When you have elicited several different answers, ask: *Do all of you like to do the same things? Is everyone good at the same things?*

2 **Building Background Knowledge:** Introduce the idea of recognizing and accepting individual differences.

- Tell students they will play a game to help them find out more about each other. They will learn some ways they are alike and some ways they are different. Explain that this game involves greeting their classmates and finding out what they like.

- Have students open their Interactive Student Notebooks to Preview 2. Read the directions for using the survey chart as students follow along.

- Model how using the pictures in the chart can help with reading the questions. Have students write their own answers (yes or no) in the *"Me"* column as you read each question.

- Explain that everyone will move about the room, asking classmates these same questions. They should continue asking questions of one person until they hear a yes answer. The classmate who answered yes to a question should write his or her name in the chart. Students should then move on to interview someone else. Emphasize that when the game chart is filled in, it should show the name of a different classmate for each question.

- Help two students model the activity. Then allow students to circulate, finding classmates to sign their game charts.

- Debrief the game. Ask students to look at their game charts to compare responses, looking for someone who answered yes to a question they answered yes to as well. Ask: *Who answered a question the same as you? How are you the same?* Then have students look at their game charts to find someone who answered a question differently from them. Ask: *Who answered a question differently from you? How are you different? Can you be friends with that person even though you are different? Why?*

3 **Developing Vocabulary:** Cover New Ideas—*alike, different,* and *learn*—as they arise in the text. You may want to discuss some terms before beginning the activity, using methods described in *Solutions for Effective Instruction.*

Social Studies Skill Builder

Phase 1: Identifying Individual Preferences and Talents

Information Master 2

1 **Discuss ways people are alike and different.** Play CD Track 2, "We Are Special." (Lyrics appear on *Information Master 2: We Are Special.*) Ask questions of individual students to prompt a discussion of how they are each special: *What do you like to do? What do you think you do best? Does everyone like to do the same things? Is everyone good at the same things? What can we learn from each other?*

   • Use pages 12 and 13 of the Big Book to review the New Ideas: *alike, different, learn.* Call attention to the illustration. Ask: *How are these children alike? How are they different? What things do you think these children are learning?*

   • Read aloud Sections 2.1–2.4 in the Big Book. Encourage students to respond to the text by looking carefully at the pictures and answering the questions on each page. (**Note:** Throughout this lesson, lead students to understand the concept of accepting one another while appreciating individual differences. This idea is implicit in this lesson, but students may need help grasping the abstraction *accept others.*)

2 **Distribute the first page of *Student Handout 2A: All About Me* as a personal interest inventory.** Remind the class that each of us likes to do different things, so everyone's answers on this sheet will be different.

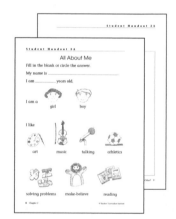

Student Handout 2A

   • As students follow along, guide them through the directions. For the last part, give other examples for each icon to help students develop a broader understanding of each area of interest. That is, they must understand that each object is a symbol of many things. For example:

   Art: not just painting, but also coloring, drawing, working with clay, building things, making jewelry, sewing

   Music: playing an instrument (not just the fiddle, but piano, tambourine, drums, xylophone, maracas, and so forth), singing, listening to music, humming along with recorded music

   Talking: expressing yourself in words; feeling comfortable in a group, not shy about speaking to others; willing to share stories about your life

   Athletics: playing a sport (not just soccer, but any kind of sport—baseball, softball, football, table tennis), dancing, doing gymnastics, swimming, riding a bike, skating, jumping rope, climbing, running

   Solving problems: counting, doing arithmetic, doing puzzles, making experiments, putting together models with many parts, playing video games

   Make-believe: not just puppets, but all forms of role-playing, dramatic playacting, putting on shows

   Reading: reading for fun; making up, telling, or writing stories

- Encourage students to circle several answers to complete the statement, *I like . . .* , but to pick only the activities they really like the best. If students have a passion that they cannot classify in one of these seven areas, help them decide what to circle. For example, if someone likes dinosaurs, ask: *Do you like to read books about dinosaurs? Do you have toy or model dinosaurs that you like to play with, making up scenes from the past?* If none of the categories seems appropriate, tell students they will have a chance to show this "like" in the next part of the activity.

3 **Have students complete the second page of Student Handout 2A to highlight their primary interest or talent.** Read the directions as students follow along. When they have finished drawing, collect the handouts for use in Phase 2 of this activity.

Phase 2: Practicing Listening and Speaking Skills

4 **Introduce the activity.** Distribute completed pages of Student Handout 2A along with the trimmed cards from *Student Handout 2B: Role Cards.* Read aloud the captions on the role cards, and model how to fold this handout along the fold line. Tell students they will use their folded role cards and Student Handout 2A as they share information about themselves with three classmates, one at a time.

5 **Model both inappropriate and appropriate ways to talk.**

- To demonstrate how to be partners for the activity, ask a student to sit with you, "face-to-face and knee-to-knee" (cross-legged) on the floor in front of the class.

- Show the "mouth" role card, and explain that you will be the Talker and share information from Student Handout 2A (use your student partner's handout). As you talk, your partner will hold up the "ear" side of his or her role card and be the Listener. Tell the class to watch for inappropriate ways that you talk to your partner.

- Model inappropriate behaviors as you share information from the handout: look away from your partner; talk very loudly, then mumble; talk very quickly; talk to another student; turn your body away from your partner.

- Debrief the role play by asking: *What did I do when I talked to my partner? How might my partner have felt when I acted this way? How should I talk?* (make eye contact, use a "six-inch voice," display positive body language, talk only to my partner)

- Now model appropriate ways to talk: make eye contact, use a normal speaking voice, sit face-to-face and knee-to-knee, talk only to your partner.

Writing Tip: Create Captions

Have students label their illustrations on Student Handout 2A, specifically identifying their favorite thing to do. Offer help with spelling as needed.

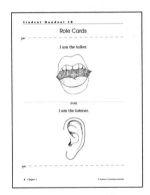

Student Handout 2B

6 Model both inappropriate and appropriate ways to listen. Choose a new volunteer to be your partner.

- Show the "ear" card and model poor listening behaviors as you listen to your partner: look away from the student, turn your body away, talk to someone else, yawn, interrupt, hum a tune.

- Debrief this role play by asking: *How might my partner have felt when I acted this way? How should I listen?* (make eye contact, sit face-to-face and knee-to-knee, use positive body language, don't talk to others, don't hum) Model all these appropriate ways to listen.

7 Arrange students in pairs for the activity. Have students bring their handouts and folded role cards and sit on the floor in two facing rows, spaced comfortably apart. Partners should sit across from one another, knee-to-knee.

8 Have students practice their talking and listening skills. Designate one row as Listeners and the other as Talkers, each holding up the appropriate role card.

- The Talkers share information about themselves from their handout for about two minutes. Circulate to observe the students' talking and listening skills. Afterward, compliment students on specific appropriate behaviors.

- Instruct students to turn over their role cards and reverse roles. Allow the new Talkers to share for two minutes.

9 Rotate partners and repeat the exercise. Have one row of students shift one position to the left so that everyone has a new partner. Repeat twice so that each student speaks and listens to three different classmates.

Phase 3: Learning from Our Similarities and Differences

10 Review this chapter's New Ideas. Project the transparency of *Information Master 2: We Are Special* and have students use these lyrics to sing along as you play CD Track 2 once again. Use pages 12 and 13 in the Big Book to review *alike* and *different*. Open the discussion by saying: *Remind me how the children in this picture are alike and how they are different.*

11 Read aloud Sections 2.1 and 2.2 in the *Social Studies Alive! My School and Family* Student Edition. Have students follow along in their books.

- As students suggest answers to the questions on each page, write words on the board for use as prompts when students work on their Reading Notes.

- Read and model the directions for Reading Notes 2 in the Interactive Student Notebook. Have students complete Parts A and B, identifying what makes them special and what they are good at doing.

12 Read aloud Sections 2.3 and 2.4 in the Student Edition as students follow along. Tell the students to remember the three classmates they shared with during the talking and listening activity, and to think about one of those classmates as they complete Parts C and D of Reading Notes 2, identifying things they can learn from one another.

13 Finish Chapter 2 by reading the Summary aloud together.

Vocabulary Development: Recognize New Words in Context

While the lyrics to "We Are Special" are projected, have students find the terms *alike*, *different*, and *learn*. Underline or highlight the words in the text. This will help students recognize the words in context and provide support for fluent reading of the lyrics.

Reading Further: The Ant's Lesson

1   **Project *Transparency 2B: The Ant's Lesson* and tell the class that it is an illustration from the story they are about to read.** Ask the following visual discovery questions to help students make some predictions about the story.

Transparency 2B

   • What do you see in this picture?

   • How are these two characters alike? How can you tell?

   • How are they different?

   • Are they doing the same things or different things?

   • What do you suppose they might learn from each other?

2   **Tell the class that the story of *The Ant's Lesson* is a retelling of a fable.** Ask: *Who knows what kind of story a fable is?* Call on volunteers to describe what they think a fable is and to name any fables they know. Explain that fables are short stories that we can learn from. Often fables have animal characters, like the ant and the grasshopper in this one. Even though the stories are about animals, they teach little lessons about life for people. The lesson is called the *moral* of the story. Ask: *What lesson do you suppose we will learn from this fable?*

3   **Open the Big Book to Reading Further 2 and read the fable aloud while students follow along.** As you read, pause to ask questions such as these:

   • What details in the picture tell you what season this is?

   • Why isn't the grasshopper worried about food? *(because there is plenty to eat in summer)*

   • What does the ant know about the seasons that the grasshopper is forgetting? *(It's hard to find food in the winter—food is scarce then—so the ant plans to store food during the summer while there is plenty to be found.)*

   • What is the lesson, or the moral, of the story?

4   **Lead students to explore the idea of the trade-offs that are involved when we make choices.** Project Transparency 2B again, and divide the class into two groups, the Ants and the Grasshoppers. Encourage them to think of themselves as part of the picture and to pantomime playing the fiddle (Grasshoppers) or carrying a heavy load (Ants). Explain that choices we make can have good sides (benefits) and bad sides (costs) to them. Ask:

   • Ants, what did you choose to do? *(to work hard to prepare for winter)* What is the good side of that choice? *(have food to eat in winter)* What is the bad side of that choice? *(not having fun during the summer)*

   • Grasshoppers, what did you choose to do? *(to play and make music all summer)* What is the good side of that choice? *(having fun all summer)* What is the bad side of that choice? *(having nothing to eat in the winter)*

5 **Help students make a connection to their own lives.** Ask:

- Have you ever had to work while someone else was playing? How did that make you feel? What was the good side of getting your work done? What was the bad side?

- What can you learn from the ant about making choices? *(Sometimes we have to think ahead about what a choice will mean for us tomorrow, and not just consider how we feel today.)*

6 **Have students open their Interactive Student Notebooks to Reading Further 2.** Read the pages aloud, one at a time, as students follow along.

- For the first page, help students finish what the grasshopper is saying in summer and in winter. Then ask students to restate the moral or lesson of the fable. They can turn to the last paragraph of the fable in the Student Edition for a model.

- On the second page, encourage students to think about the grasshopper's special gifts and what the ant could have learned from the grasshopper. As they finish what the grasshopper is saying, offer help with spelling as needed. When students have finished, ask for volunteers to share their ideas. (**Note:** Some students may already be familiar with a modern retelling of this fable, in which the grasshopper is valued for his musical talents and is invited into the ants' home to share their winter food in exchange for entertaining them.)

Processing

1 **Tell students they are going to color a gift box to celebrate a classmate's individual differences.** Arrange students in pairs for this activity.

- Have students open their Interactive Student Notebooks to Processing 2. Distribute *Student Handout 2C: A Gift to Our Class* to each student.

- Explain that the students will be coloring the wrapped gift box on Student Handout 2C to show what is special about their partner.

- Read the directions in Processing 2 as students follow along. Have them color all the crayons on the two pages to use as a color key for their work on the gift. Model the activity, showing how someone might color the gift to represent you.

- Tell students to use their listening and talking skills to find out what their partner likes to do best, then circle the matching word or picture. Remind the class that each picture is a symbol that stands for a broad range of activities, not just the item shown. The partner may identify from one to four special interests, since the gift box has four sections that could be colored differently.

Student Handout 2C

- Have students begin by writing their partner's name at the bottom of the handout. Then have them color in the gift box, choosing crayons to match those pictured above each area of interest they circled on Processing 2. If the partner has one area of interest, the entire gift will be one color; if two areas, each half will be a different color; if four areas, each fourth of the box will be a different color. If the partner chose three areas of interest, encourage students to color two squares for the area the partner likes best.

2 **Have students present their gifts to the class to show how each individual is special.**

- Call on a Presenter to stand and tell about the gift box he or she created while the partner also stands. Display *Transparency 2C: Gift Box Color Key* for reference during this discussion.

- Have the Presenter place the gift box in a designated spot, such as along the chalk tray or on a bulletin board, and say, "(Student's name) is a gift to our class."

3 **Ask students to compare and contrast the personalities represented by the collected gifts.** Have students spend some time grouping similar gift boxes together as they review how their classmates are alike and different. As the students consider everyone's special talents, encourage them to reflect again on what they could learn from one another.

Transparency 2C

Assessment

Masters for the chapter assessment appear in the *Lesson Masters.* Answers appear below.

Big Ideas

1. Answers will vary. Students may circle any item pictured.

2. color yellow: soccer ball and basketball; or two books; or two puzzle pieces (any of these similar pairs)

3. color blue: the ant

Show You Know

4. Answers will vary. Drawings should suggest a child's activity.

English Language Learners

Give English language learners a way to understand and remember the vocabulary words *alike* and *different* that are used throughout this lesson. Before beginning the lesson, help students create a two-column chart on construction paper. Label one column *same/alike* and the other *different*. Distribute stickers for students to place on the chart in pairs. Guide them to place a pair of identical stickers in the *same/alike* column, side by side, and a pair of unlike stickers in the *different* column, again side by side. Alternatively, have the students draw (or color, cut, and paste) a pair of suitable pictures for each column. Students can refer back to this simple chart throughout the lesson when they need help remembering the meanings of these words.

Students with Special Needs

To help students complete Processing 2 in their Interactive Student Notebooks, create a color key beforehand for them to follow. Be sure to choose crayons with clearly differentiated versions of each color that a student will easily recognize. If possible, let the students do their coloring with the same crayons that you used to make the key. Have students color the gift to represent themselves (rather than a partner) and then share their work with a friend or partner. Both adjustments will help students complete the activity in the allotted time.

Enrichment

Your class might enjoy acting out the fable of *The Ant's Lesson* as a short play or as Reader's Theater. Assign different speaking roles, and for a play, encourage students to create their own simple props and costumes. Consider adding a narrator whose role is to comment on aspects of the play that relate directly to concepts discussed in this chapter (*alike, differences, learn, making choices*).

Enrichment Resources

Have students find out more about individual differences by exploring the following Enrichment Resources for *Social Studies Alive! My School and Family* at www.learntci.com.

Internet Connections

These recommended Web sites provide useful and engaging content that enforces skills development and mastery of subjects within the chapter.

Enrichment Readings

These in-depth readings encourage students to explore selected topics related to the chapter. For Chapter 2, you may wish to use one or more of the Enrichment Readings listed for the chapter. You may also find readings that relate the chapter's content directly to your state's curriculum.

Additional Reading Opportunities

These books, which can be read aloud to students, offer opportunities to extend the content in this chapter.

Elmer by David McKee (New York: HarperCollins, 1989)

Elmer, a colorful patchwork elephant, wants to look like all the other elephants. In the end, Elmer realizes that he is most comfortable just being himself. This story conveys an important message about the value of individual differences.

The McElderry Book of Aesop's Fables by Michael Morpurgo. Illustrated by Emma Chichester Clark. (New York: Margaret K. McElderry Books, 2005)

This illustrated version of Aesop's fables retells 21 of the original tales in lively, conversational language that makes them especially good read-alouds.

My Friends/Mis Amigos by Taro Gomi (San Francisco: Chronicle Books, 2006)

A young girl learns from her animal friends how to hop, jump, march, and more. The repetitive phrase, "I learned to _____ from my friend the _____," supports beginning readers and provides a model for students' own writing about learning from their friends.

Ruby the Copycat by Peggy Rathmann (New York: Scholastic, 1997)

Ruby keeps copying everything Angela does, which makes the other children in class angry. A patient and understanding teacher helps Ruby to discover her own creativity. This story encourages students to dare to be themselves and explore their own talents.

It is summer. What is the grasshopper doing?

I am _Answers may vary. Possible answers:_
singing, dancing, playing, having fun .

Now it is winter. How does the grasshopper feel?

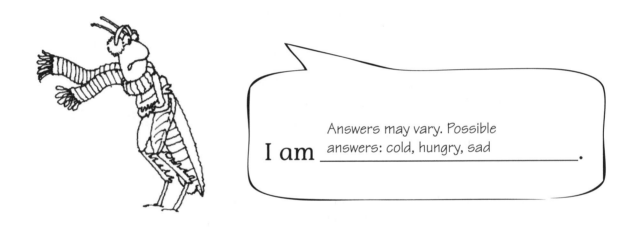

I am _Answers may vary. Possible_
answers: cold, hungry, sad .

What did the grasshopper learn from the ant?

Look in your book to find the lesson.

There is a time to work and a time to play. Always think about tomorrow.

Think of a different lesson.

Let's say the ant learned from the grasshopper.

The grasshopper was good at something.

What was it? What could the ant have learned?

Answers may vary.

I am good at <u>making music</u>.

I can help you learn <u>how to make music, sing, dance,</u>

<u>and have fun</u>.

Why Do Schools Have Rules?

Overview

Students learn about the reasons for having rules. In the Preview, students talk about familiar rules at home and at school. In an Experiential Exercise, they play a game without rules to discover why rules are needed. They then read about four reasons for school rules and talk about the consequences of not following them. In Reading Further, students discover that cities also have rules and that city leaders talk and vote to make new rules. In the Processing activity, they illustrate one classroom rule and the consequences of breaking it.

Objectives

Social Studies

- Identify the purpose and benefits of having rules at school.
- Compare rules at home with rules at school.
- Vote to make a decision.
- Illustrate the consequences of following and breaking rules.

Language Arts

- Contribute to group discussions. (speaking and listening)
- Write and illustrate one school rule. (writing)

Social Studies Vocabulary

get along, be safe, be fair, learn

Materials

Social Studies Alive! My School and Family Big Book and Student Editions

Transparencies 3A and 3B

Interactive Student Notebooks

kick balls or soccer balls

cone or other marker for a relay race

Time Estimates

Preview: 30 min.

Experiential Exercise: 2 sessions (30 min. each)

Reading Further: 30 min.

Processing: 30 min.

Activity	Suggested Time	Materials
Preview • Connecting to Prior Knowledge • Building Background Knowledge • Developing Vocabulary	30 minutes	• *Social Studies Alive! My School and Family* Big Book, Chapter 3 introduction • Interactive Student Notebooks
Experiential Exercise Identifying the value of rules for group settings	30-minute sessions (2) • Discovering the reason for rules (Steps 1–5) • Reading about school rules (Steps 6–8)	• *Social Studies Alive! My School and Family* Big Book and Student Editions, Sections 3.1—3.4 • Transparency 3A • Interactive Student Notebooks • kick balls or soccer balls (2 for the class) • cone or other marker for relay race
Reading Further Exploring the process of rule-making for a city	30 minutes	• *Social Studies Alive! My School and Family* Big Book, Chapter 3 Reading Further • Transparency 3B • Interactive Student Notebooks
Processing Writing and illustrating a school rule and the results of not following it	30 minutes	• Interactive Student Notebooks
Assessment	15 minutes	• Chapter 3 Assessment, Lesson Masters • Chapter 3 Assessment, Digital Teacher Resources

Preview

1 **Connecting to Prior Knowledge:** Invite the students to think about rules they have at home, perhaps related to bedtime, behavior at meals, or the use of other people's belongings. Allow them to talk briefly in small groups, sharing ideas about their families' rules.

- Have students open their Interactive Student Notebooks to Preview 3 and draw a picture to show a family rule in their home.

- When students have finished, ask for volunteers to share their answers.

- To get students thinking about how rules are made, ask: *Who makes the rules in your home?*

2 **Building Background Knowledge:** Use the *Social Studies Alive! My School and Family* Big Book to introduce the concept of rules at school. Open to Chapter 3 and read the title aloud.

- Call attention to the three illustrations on these pages. Ask: *What do you see?* Point to the lunchroom scene and ask: *Where is this taking place?* Repeat this question for the scenes at the art table and the play center. Then ask: *What rules might the children be following in the lunchroom? At the art table? In the play center?*

3 **Developing Vocabulary:** Cover New Ideas—*get along, be safe, be fair,* and *learn*—as they arise in the text. You may want to discuss some terms before beginning the activity, using methods described in *Solutions for Effective Instruction.*

Experiential Exercise

1 **Take students outdoors or to the multipurpose room and introduce the activity.** Tell them they will now play a game that is lots of fun. Explain the game quickly: there are two teams, each team gets a ball, and the fastest team wins. Be evasive when students ask for clarification. (**Note:** The point of the game is for the students to discover the need for rules; thus, give them as little direction as possible.) When pressed for a game objective, simply repeat: *Remember, the fastest team wins.*

2 **Have students play the game.** Put the two balls on the ground, and remind players that the fastest team wins. Tell them to begin the game. Expect some students to be excited and energetic and others to be concerned and confused. Provide no other rules or direction.

3 **Stop the game and debrief the experience.** Ask such questions as:

- How did you feel?

- Was this a good game? Why or why not?

- How could this be a better game?

When students express frustration and confusion, encourage them to state what was "missing" from the game. Respond by agreeing that the game was not very satisfying because there were no rules to guide the players. Tell them they will play the game again, following these rules:

- For an outdoor game: Conduct a two-team relay race; one runner runs around a cone and back, handing the ball to the next runner.

- For an indoor game: Conduct a two-team relay race; players pass the ball between their legs to the next player, up the line, and then back again.

4 **Have students play the game, following the rules you gave.** Observe the race. Expect the students to be much more controlled, more focused, and less anxious than when they played the game with no rules.

5 **Stop the game and debrief the experience.** Ask such questions as:

- How did you feel this time?

- Which game did you like better?

- Where else do rules help us?

- Do you think it is important to have rules at school? Why or why not?

- Can you name one of our school (or classroom) rules?

6 **Help students identify the purpose and benefits of rules.** To discuss the New Ideas *get along, be safe, be fair,* and *learn,* project *Transparency 3A: Why Do Schools Have Rules?* Ask volunteers to come up and point to one of the scenes as they answer questions like the following:

- Where do you see children getting along? What are they doing?

- Where do you see children being safe? What might they do that is not safe?

- Where do you see children being fair? What are they doing?

- Where do you see children learning? What might they be learning?

Then turn through Sections 3.1–3.4 in the Big Book. Encourage the class to talk briefly about the pictures and answer the question on each page. Ask from time to time: *What might happen if someone broke that rule?*

7 **Have the students identify school rules that involve helping everyone get along.**

- Read aloud Section 3.1 in the *Social Studies Alive! My School and Family* Student Edition as students follow along in their books.

- Ask students what the rule "We are kind" means to them. As needed, prompt them with situations you have seen in class, including both courteous and unkind behaviors for them to characterize.

- If you have already established class rules, ask the students to identify which of your rules are intended to help everyone get along. Talk about any procedures you have for dealing with conflicts. You might discuss, for example, being truthful, being considerate of others' feelings, using good manners, and dealing with anger and disagreements.

- Ask: *Does your family have rules for getting along with each other? Which ones are like our class rules? Which ones are different?*

Transparency 3A

Speaking and Listening: Give Concrete Examples

While discussing abstract ideas such as *get along* and *be kind*, prompt students to give concrete, detailed examples from their personal experience. To reinforce listening skills, ask another student to repeat or paraphrase each example.

- Have students open their Interactive Student Notebooks to Reading Notes 3. Read and model the directions on page 16. Call on volunteers to talk about the two pictures and how they are different. Have students circle the picture that shows all three children getting along. Then talk about the other picture. Ask: *What rule is being broken?* (The "sharing" rule: let everone play.) *What happens when people break this rule?* (The girl who is left out has her feelings hurt.) *How should the children resolve this conflict?* (The two playing the game could invite the girl to join them; the girl who is left out could ask politely if she may play, too.)

8 Have the students identify school rules that involve keeping everyone safe.

- Read aloud Section 3.2 of the Student Edition as students follow along. Have them relate the rules in the text to the photographs on the page.

- Help students identify the rules at your school that are designed to keep them safe—in traffic, on the playground, in the halls, in the classroom, and in special situations, such as when the alarm rings for a fire drill.

- Ask: *Does your family have rules for being safe at home? Which rules are like our class rules? Which ones are different?*

- Guide students in completing page 17 of Reading Notes 3. After students have selected the picture where the children are being safe, ask: *In the other picture, what rule is being broken?* (Don't pass scissors with the point toward someone.) *What could happen?* (The person taking the scissors could get hurt.)

9 Have the students identify school rules that involve fairness.

- Read aloud Section 3.3 of the Student Edition and discuss.

- Ask for examples of the types of rules that support fairness; for example, playing by the rules of games (not cheating), being honest with one another, listening to each side of a conflict, not placing blame carelessly, allowing everyone a chance to participate, sharing class supplies or playground equipment, taking equal turns, or cleaning up after yourself.

- Guide students in completing page 18 of Reading Notes 3. After students have selected the picture where the children are being fair, ask: *In the other picture, what rule is being broken?* (Share the blocks fairly with anyone who wants to play.) *What happens?* (The girl feels sad because she doesn't have enough blocks.)

10 Have the students identify school rules that involve helping everyone learn.

- Read aloud Section 3.4 of the Student Edition and discuss.

- Help students identify those classroom rules that give everyone a chance to learn; for example, raising your hand and waiting to be called on, listening quietly while others are speaking, doing your own work, working quietly, or finishing your work before you begin to do something else.

- Guide students in completing page 19 of Reading Notes 3. After students have selected the picture where the children are learning, ask: *In the other picture, what rule is being broken?* (Don't play with your own toys during class time.) *What happens when you do that?* (You aren't learning, and you may be bothering classmates who are doing their work.)

11 **Discuss briefly who makes the school rules.** Some rules, for example, may be set by the principal or by the local school board. If you have involved your students in setting up your classroom rules, help them recognize that they had a hand in making the rules for their class.

Reading Further: Let's Vote on It

1 **Project *Transparency 3B: City Hall.*** Cover the title. Ask the following visual discovery questions to help the students analyze the photograph and make some predictions.

- What do you see in this picture?

- What can you tell about this room? Where do you think it might be located?

- What do you think usually happens in this room?

- What do you suppose the children are doing here?

2 **Tell the class that this room is in the City Hall in Bellflower, California.** Explain that they are going to read about a field trip that a class of second graders took to City Hall, where the rules for their city are made.

3 **Read aloud the text on Big Book pages 28–29 and discuss it with students.**

- Help the class understand that when the children acted out a city meeting, it was like doing role plays in your class—except that these Bellflower children went to City Hall, so their play-acting seems very real.

- Explain that every city has a place like this where the city leaders meet. Usually the mayor (the head of the city) and the city council members (people who are elected to represent the people in the city) sit up at the front of the room, behind the big desk. People from the city can come and sit in the seats that fill the rest of the room. They listen to the leaders talk, and sometimes they speak up to let the city leaders know how they feel about things, because the leaders' job is to serve all the people in the city.

- Ask if anyone can guess what the city leaders do. (*It is their job to run the city, make city rules, and help the people who live in the city.*)

4 **Continue reading pages 30–31 in the Big Book.** As you read, pause to talk about the ideas the Bellflower children discussed:

- What is the problem with riding bikes on the sidewalk? What is the problem with riding bikes in the street?

Transparency 3B

- What was the children's idea for how to solve both problems?

- What does it mean when it says the leaders *voted* on it? *(Be sure students understand that voting is a way for a group to make a choice or a decision.)*

- When a group votes, how do you know which side wins?

5 **After reading page 31 in the Big Book, further discuss voting.** Ask students what kinds of things they think they will get to vote for when they turn 18.

- Discuss the phrase, *the right to vote.* Help students understand the word *right* as meaning something people are free to do according to the laws of the United States. Introduce the term *domocracy* as a kind of government in which decisions are made by the people through voting. The United States is a democracy. Ask: *Is the city of Bellflower a democracy? Could we call our class a democracy?*

- Ask the students for examples of voting they may have done in class. For example, do you sometimes ask for a show of hands to see which book the class wants to have read or what they want to do for recess on a rainy day? Guide them to explain how they know which side wins. (That is, each raised hand is a "vote," and the side with the most hands—or votes—wins.) Ask: *Why is voting a fair way to decide?*

- Help students understand that in a city, the city leaders sometimes vote to make a rule for the people, the way the children of Bellflower did in their role-playing. Other times, everyone in the city gets to vote. Both are forms of democracy.

6 **Demonstrate the difference between direct and representative democracy.** Have students vote to make a decision, using each form in succession: one-person/one-vote (direct democracy) and a vote conducted by our leaders (representative democracy).

- Choose an issue for a quick class vote, using an idea that you are willing to carry out according to the students' decision. For example, "Which would you rather do for snack time: go outside, or stay inside and listen to music?" Write the choices on the board, and let students come up and mark an X by their choice. Help them count the votes to decide the winning choice.

- Next, quickly divide the class into four or five groups and ask each group to choose a leader. Members of each group should let their leader know their preference for the class vote. Present the same choices again, but this time allow only the leaders to come and mark their vote on the board. Discuss whether the result of the vote is the same, and in what situations it might be easier to have only our leaders vote. Explain that many decisions that are made by our government are made by leaders we have voted for.

7 **Have students open their Interactive Student Notebooks to Reading Further 3.** Read the pages aloud, one at a time, as students follow along.

- After students have completed the first page, ask for volunteers to read the two rules that the children of Bellflower voted for in their meeting.

- On the second page, read aloud the sign "Use Bike Lane" and the reason for that rule. Spend a moment with the class brainstorming other rules for being safe on city streets. Write a few of their ideas on the board. Then have the students illustrate one of these rules.

Processing

1 **Create a chart of your classroom and school rules.** On the board or chart paper, set up a four-column chart. Write one of the four New Ideas at the top of each column. Ask questions such as the following to prompt the students for rules that involve the first two New Ideas, *get along* and *be safe*, and record their responses on the chart.

- What rules help us *get along* in our classroom? *(We share, we talk and listen, we take turns.)*

- What rules help us *be safe* in our classroom? *(We don't run, we don't stand on furniture, we don't throw things, we keep things picked up so people don't trip over them.)*

Continue the discussion for rules that help us *be fair* and *learn*. (**Note:** Students may suggest overlapping rules for the four categories because many classroom rules support more than one of these ideas. Allow all appropriate responses. Help the students understand the reasons for any rules they perceive as arbitrary.)

2 **Have students illustrate the consequences of following and breaking a rule.** Ask students to open their Interactive Student Notebooks to Processing 3. Read the directions as they follow along. Have them write a school rule that is listed on your four-column chart and then draw pictures to illustrate examples of what happens when that rule is followed and when it is broken. Follow up with a discussion of the consequences of breaking a rule.

Assessment

Masters for the chapter assessment appear in the *Lesson Masters*. Answers appear below.

Big Ideas

1. biking with helmet: Rules help us be safe.

   raising hands in class: Rules help us learn.

   passing out crayons: Rules help us be fair.

2. rules

Show You Know

3. Answers will vary. Possible answer: Be nice. The drawing should match the student's written rule.

English Language Learners

While doing the Building Background Knowledge activity, be aware that children from other countries may not be familiar with these different regions of a school (lunchroom, art table, play center). Ask them to name any items in the pictures that they do recognize in order to help them build on what they know.

Students with Special Needs

As you work to develop vocabulary throughout the lesson, use role-playing to enhance comprehension of the four New Ideas: *get along, be safe, be fair,* and *learn.* For each idea, choose volunteers to act out two simple scenes, representing the term and its opposite. For example, for *get along,* the teacher might have two students act out happily sharing a classroom item, such as crayons, and then act out selfishly *not* sharing the same item. Discuss facial expressions, body language, and the words that people use as they practice getting along, being safe, being fair, and learning. This will give the children a visual and kinesthetic memory of the meaning of each new term.

In the Experiential Exercise, modify the game to accommodate children with physical disabilities. For example, you might play the game indoors and establish the rule that players remain seated as they quickly pass the ball from hand to hand, without throwing it.

Enrichment

Start a student council for your classroom, and allow the class to vote for leaders. Officers might include a President, Vice President, Director of Supplies, and Recess Coordinator. Arrange a time for this council to meet to discuss and set three classroom rules. Provide banner or poster paper and help the council members create a large display for each rule, with words and pictures. When the council presents the rules to the class, have the rest of the students role-play what each rule looks like. Encourage students to tell one another each time they see someone following one of these rules.

Enrichment Resources

Have students find out more about rules and laws by exploring the following Enrichment Resources for *Social Studies Alive! My School and Family* at www.learntci.com.

Internet Connections

These recommended Web sites provide useful and engaging content that enforces skills development and mastery of subjects within the chapter.

Enrichment Readings

These in-depth readings encourage students to explore selected topics related to the chapter. For Chapter 3, you may wish to use one or more of the Enrichment Readings listed for the chapter. You may also find readings that relate the chapter's content directly to your state's curriculum.

Additional Reading Opportunities

The following books, which can be read aloud to students, offer opportunities to extend the content in this chapter.

After School Rules by David Kirk (New York: Grosset and Dunlap, 2006)
When a little spider, ant, and grasshopper disagree about what game to play after school, they must find a solution that keeps everyone happy. This picture book helps students understand how to make rules so that everyone can get along.

Bonaparte by Marsha Wilson Chall. Illustrated by Wendy Anderson Halperin. (New York: Dorling Kindersley, 2000)
Young Jean Claude goes away to boarding school and must leave his dog Bonaparte behind. Finally, Jean Claude persuades the administration to change the school rules so that dogs will be allowed. Students should enjoy this humorous portrayal of the importance of school rules.

Peanut's Emergency by Cristina Salat. Illustrated by Tammie Lyon. (Watertown, MA: Charlesbridge Publishing, 2002)
Unaware that her mother's car has broken down, a little girl is left at school with no way home. Peanut must remember the safety rules she has been taught and figure out where to get help so she can get home safely.

What's a City Council? by Nancy Harris (Portsmouth, NH: Heinemann, 2007)
This book helps young readers understand the duties of city council members and their role in making city laws. It provides another look at the world that the children of Bellflower discovered at their City Hall.

Where are all the children getting along?

Circle the picture.

Where are the children being safe?

Circle the picture.

Where are the children being fair?

Circle the picture.

Where are the children learning?

Circle the picture.

These children had a meeting at City Hall.

They voted for two rules. Circle the two rules.

• Dogs must be on a leash.

• Anyone on a bike must use the bike lane.

• No one can set off fireworks.

• Do not run in the halls.

• Children on bikes must wear helmets.

Who Helps Us at School?

Overview

Students learn about the typical duties of a school teacher, principal, secretary, and custodian and discover how each contributes to the school community. In the Preview, students consider people who help them in their own school. In a Visual Discovery activity, they analyze photographs of school staff and listen to a recording of each person describing his or her job. They use this information to act out each role. In Reading Further, they learn about someone else whose job is to help the community—a Congresswoman. In the Processing activity, students create a class book about the people who help them at school.

Objectives

Social Studies

- Make inferences about a person's job from visual images.
- Give supporting evidence for inferences.
- Identify the contributions of service providers in the school.
- Identify the contributions of leaders in our government.

Language Arts

- Acquire information from an oral narrative. (listening)
- Give appropriate answers in a mock interview. (speaking)
- Illustrate pages for a class book describing the jobs of people at school. (writing)

Social Studies Vocabulary

teacher, principal, secretary, custodian

Materials

Social Studies Alive! My School and Family Big Book and Student Editions

Transparencies 4A–4F

Interactive Student Notebooks

Lesson Masters

- Information Masters 4A–4F
- Student Handouts 4A–4N

CD Tracks 3–6

stickers

Time Estimates

Preview: 10 min.

Visual Discovery:

5 sessions (30 min. each)

Reading Further: 35 min.

Processing: 30 min.

Activity	Suggested Time	Materials
Preview • Connecting to Prior Knowledge • Building Background Knowledge • Developing Vocabulary	10 minutes	• Interactive Student Notebooks
Visual Discovery Identifying and dramatizing some roles and responsibilities of adults who work in the school	*Phase 1* 30-minute sessions (4) • Teacher (Steps 1–5) • Principal (Step 6–9) • Secretary (Steps 10–13) • Custodian (Steps 14–17) *Phase 2* 30-minute session • Who Am I? riddles (Steps 18–20)	• Transparencies 4A–4D • Information Masters 4A–4F (1 transparency each of 4B and 4E) • Student Handouts 4A and 4B (cut apart, 1 prop per student) • CD Tracks 3–6 • stickers (4 per pair, in two colors) • *Social Studies Alive! My School and Family* Big Book and Student Editions, Sections 4.1–4.4 • Transparency 4E • Interactive Student Notebooks
Reading Further Outlining some roles and responsibilities of our public servants	35 minutes	• *Social Studies Alive! My School and Family* Big Book, Chapter 4 Reading Further • Transparency 4F • Interactive Student Notebooks • U.S. wall map (optional)
Processing Creating a class book of school jobs	30 minutes	• Interactive Student Notebooks • Student Handouts 4C–4N (1 sheet per student; 2 sets for a class of 24)
Assessment	15 minutes	• Chapter 4 Assessment, Lesson Masters • Chapter 4 Assessment, Digital Teacher Resources

Preview

1   **Connecting to Prior Knowledge:** Help students identify the adults who help them at their school.

- Have students open their Interactive Student Notebooks to Preview 4. Read the directions aloud while students follow along.

- Remind the class that many grown-ups help them at school in different ways. Ask: *Who helps you at school? How does that person help you?*

- Put students into mixed-ability pairs to discuss their ideas for a few minutes. Then have each student draw one example of who helps them at school. Tell them to give you a "thumbs up" when they are ready to share.

- Have pairs share their answers with the class. List their ideas on the board.

2   **Building Background Knowledge:** Briefly introduce the term *service job.* When a person has a job that involves helping others, we say that the person is providing a service. Explain that each person the students drew in their Preview 4 has a service job. Tell the class that in this chapter, they will learn more about what it means to have a service job in a school.

3   **Developing Vocabulary:** Cover the New Ideas—*teacher, principal, secretary,* and *custodian*—as they arise in the text. You may want to discuss some terms before beginning the activity, using methods described in *Solutions for Effective Instruction.*

Visual Discovery

Phase 1: Identifying Roles and Responsibilities in the School

1   **Put students in mixed-ability pairs to make inferences about a teacher's role and responsibilities.** Tell the class that you will show a picture of a person. You want the students to be detectives and look for clues in the picture to try to figure out the person's job.

2   **Project *Transparency 4A: The Teacher.*** Cover the title. Ask:

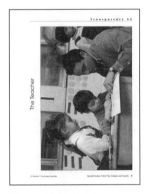

Transparency 4A

- What clues do you see?

- Who do you think this person might be?

- What clues helped you decide?

- What do you think this teacher is doing? (Ask for evidence to support the answer.)

- What other things do you think a teacher does to help you at school?

3 **Tell the class they will now listen to this teacher talk about his job.** Encourage students to listen closely to all the things the teacher does to help at school. Also tell them to listen for things the teacher will ask them to do. For each interactive question in the script, model the actions for students. Play CD Track 3, "I Am a Teacher." (**Note:** The script is provided on *Information Master 4A: I Am a Teacher.*) Repeat the track as many times as needed. Afterward, ask the questions below. Allow pairs a few minutes to discuss each question. Then call on volunteers to share their answers.

- What did you learn about this teacher?
- What does this teacher teach his students?
- What does this teacher do to help students' families?
- What does this teacher do to take care of his students?

4 **Prepare students for the "interview" act-it-outs.** Explain that students will be acting out the ways a teacher helps students and their families.

- Model this example of an act-it-out: Two students stand in front of the transparency image to act out how this teacher is helping children in this class. One student acts as the teacher; the other acts as the child being helped.
- Cluster pairs into three groups. Assign each group a different role:

  something a teacher does to teach children

  something a teacher does to help families

  something a teacher does to help children get along
- Project a transparency of *Information Master 4B: Interview Act-It-Outs.* Explain that you will act as a reporter. You will interview the "teachers" by asking three questions. Read aloud the questions on the transparency as students follow along.

5 **Have students perform the interview act-it-outs to identify the contributions of a teacher to the school community.** Direct pairs from the first group to position themselves to "step into the scene." Have pairs take turns acting and being interviewed. Repeat the steps of the interview act-it-outs with the remaining two groups: something a teacher does to help families and something a teacher does to help children get along.

Speaking and Listening: Listen for Information

After students listen to the teacher tell about what he does, have them make a quick sketch to represent some part of the job as he described it. This will help them be prepared to talk about what they heard. (Repeat for each CD track in this activity.)

Information Master 4A

I Am a Teacher

Hello. My name is Mr. Hayes. I am a first grade teacher at Seacastle Elementary School. I love being a teacher! Let me tell you what I do.

I bet you have already guessed my most important job. That's right! I teach my students all sorts of new things. Every morning, I'm in the classroom by 8 o'clock, ready to greet my students. Some of them give me a "high five" as they come in the room. Can you show me a high five?

We start class right away, because we have a lot to learn. Every day we have lessons in reading and math. I love teaching social studies. I also teach a great science lesson about frogs. Raise your hand if you like frogs as much as I do!

My students really want to do well in school. When they turn in their papers, I check their work. I draw a smiley face on each paper. Can you draw a big smiley face in the air? Then my first graders take the papers home to show their families. Parents always want to know, "How is my child doing in school?" So I talk to moms and dads on the phone, or meet them at school. That's a big part of my job.

It's also my job to make sure my students get along in my classroom. I help them learn the best ways to behave. Do they know how to share and take turns? Do they know how to talk and listen? Do they know the rules? If two students are having problems with each other, we step outside the room. I help them work things out.

I like to help my students learn. I like talking to their families. I like making sure that everyone in my class is happy and safe.

© Teachers' Curriculum Institute Who Helps Us at School? 15

Information Master 4A

Information Master 4B

Interview Act-It-Outs

Practice your act-it-out.

Answer these questions:

- Who are you?
- What are you doing?
- How do you help at your school?

16 Chapter 4 © Teachers' Curriculum Institute

Information Master 4B

6 Put students in mixed-ability pairs to make inferences about the principal's role and responsibilities.

7 Project *Transparency 4B: The Principal,* covering the title. Ask:

- What clues do you see?

- Who do you think this person might be?

- What clues helped you decide?

- What do you think this school principal is doing? (Ask for evidence to support the answer.)

- What other things do you think a principal does to help at school?

Transparency 4B

8 Play CD Track 4, "I Am a Principal." (Refer to *Information Master 4C: I Am a Principal* for the script.) Again, alert students to listen for things the principal will ask them to do. As the CD plays, model responses to the interactive questions. Replay the CD track as needed. Allow pairs a few minutes to discuss the questions below, then ask volunteers to share their answers.

- What did you learn about this principal?

- What does this principal do to help students?

- What does this principal do to help students' families?

- What does this principal do to help teachers?

Information Master 4C

9 Prepare students for the interview act-it-outs in which they identify a principal's contributions to the school community.

- Project Information Master 4B again and review the interview act-it-out directions.

- Cluster pairs into three groups. Assign each group a different role to act out:

  something a principal does to help students

  something a principal does to help families

  something a principal does to help teachers

- Explain that you will act as a reporter as you did before. Have students perform the interview act-it-outs, following the procedure in Step 5.

10 Put students in mixed-ability pairs to make inferences about the school secretary's role and responsibilities. Project *Transparency 4C: The School Secretary,* covering the title, and ask the same series of questions:

- What clues do you see?

- Who do you think this person might be?

- What clues helped you decide?

- What do you think this school secretary is doing? (Ask for evidence to support the answer.)

- What other things do you think a school secretary does to help at school?

Transparency 4C

11 Play CD Track 5, "I Am a School Secretary." (Refer to *Information Master 4D: I Am a School Secretary* for the script.) As the interactive questions arise, model the actions for students. Replay the track as needed. Ask:

- What did you find out about this school secretary?

- How does this school secretary use a telephone to do her job? A computer? A smile?

- How does this school secretary help at her school?

12 Prepare students to perform "talking statue" act-it-outs in which they play the role of a secretary on the job at school.

- Cluster pairs into three groups. Assign each group a different role:

  a secretary talking on the phone (prop: phone)

  a secretary working at a computer (prop: computer)

  a secretary greeting a visitor (prop: smile)

- Distribute the props cut from *Student Handout 4A: Secretary Props* to the appropriate group. Give each student his or her own copy of the prop.

- Tell students that only one partner from each pair will come up to the front of the class to be a statue. Each pair should work together planning how the statue will move and what the statue will say, so that either one of them is prepared to act as the talking statue. Show them where the actors will stand in front of the transparency image.

- Project a transparency of *Information Master 4E: Talking Statue Act-It-Outs*, and go over the general directions with the class.

- Distribute two stickers to each pair, one for the statue's "move" button and the other for the "talk" button. Explain that to be a talking statue, a student puts one sticker on his or her right shoulder and then "freezes" like a statue until someone presses this "move" button. Allow time for students to practice their act-it-outs.

- Explain that a talking statue also has a "talk" button on the left shoulder. When someone presses this button, the statue can speak. Read aloud the three points on Information Master 4E that describe what a statue will say. Allow time for students to practice what they will say as a talking statue.

13 Have students perform talking statue act-it-outs to identify a secretary's contributions to the school community.

- Choose three students with telephone props to stand in front of the screen. Tell them to "freeze" into the role of the school secretary.

- Invite a student from the audience to press one statue's "move" button, allowing that statue to act. Have the class guess what the secretary statue is doing.

Information Master 4D

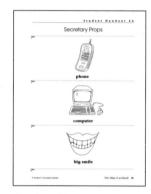

Student Handout 4A

Information Master 4E

- Next invite a student from the audience to press the same statue's "talk" button, allowing the secretary statue to explain what she is doing and how she helps at school.

- Give each secretary-on-the-phone statue a chance to move and talk at the push of a button.

- Repeat for the remaining two statues: secretary working at a computer, and secretary greeting a visitor.

14 Put students in mixed-ability pairs to make inferences about the school custodian's role and responsibilities. Project *Transparency 4D: The School Custodian,* covering the title, and ask the same series of questions:

- What clues do you see?

- Who do you think this person might be?

- What clues helped you decide?

- What do you think this school custodian is doing? (Ask for evidence to support the answer.)

- What other things do you think a custodian does to help at school?

15 Play CD Track 6, "I Am a School Custodian." (For the script, see *Information Master 4F: I Am a School Custodian.*) Model responses to the interactive questions. Replay the CD track as needed. Ask:

- What did you find out about this school custodian?

- What does he do before school?

- What does he do during school?

- What does he do after school?

16 Prepare students for the talking statue act-it-outs in which they play the role of a custodian on the job at school.

- Project Information Master 4E again and review the directions.

- Cluster pairs into three groups. Assign each group a different role:

  something a custodian does before school (prop: key)

  something a custodian does during school (prop: paintbrush)

  something a custodian does after school (prop: mop)

- Distribute the props cut from *Student Handout 4B: Custodian Props* to the appropriate group. Give each student his or her own copy of the prop.

17 Have students perform the talking statue act-it-outs to identify a custodian's contributions to the school community. Follow the procedure described for secretary act-it-outs in Step 13.

Transparency 4D

Information Master 4F

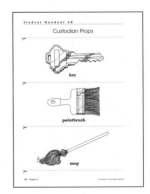

Student Handout 4B

Phase 2: Reviewing Roles and Making Inferences

18 Review the jobs of teacher, principal, secretary, and custodian. Use *Transparency 4E: Who Helps Us at School?* or the picture in the Big Book to reinforce the New Ideas: *teacher, principal, secretary,* and *custodian.*

- Remind the class that these are all *service jobs.* As students consider each of the four scenes, ask *Where might this scene be taking place? What clues tell you who is in this scene? What do you think these people are doing?*

- Read aloud Sections 4.1 through 4.4 in the Big Book. Encourage students to respond to the text by looking at the pictures and answering the riddle on each page.

19 Read aloud the Summary as students follow along.

- Ask volunteers to name one helper at your school who has a service job and to tell some of the services that person provides. Repeat until students have described several school jobs.

- Call attention to the importance of these school figures with such questions as these: *What do you think would happen if the classroom didn't have a teacher? What might happen if the school didn't have a principal?*

20 Have students answer riddles as they continue to make inferences about the roles of adults who help them at school. Tell them to open their Interactive Student Notebooks to Reading Notes 4. Read the directions aloud and model each activity. First have students match the pictures of school employees with words from the Word Bank. Then read the riddles aloud and have students match each riddle with the appropriate school helper. Remind students to look at Sections 4.1–4.4 in their Student Editions as they complete Reading Notes 4.

Reading Further: Ms. Johnson Has Many Jobs

1 Project *Transparency 4F: Eddie Bernice Johnson* and tell the class that they are going to learn about this woman and her job. Ask the following visual discovery questions to help students make some predictions.

- What do you see in these pictures?

- Do you think this woman is someone who helps at a school? What clues are you using to decide?

- What do you think this building is?

- Do you think the woman might work in this building? If she does work here, what do you think her job could be?

If none of the students has recognized the Capitol building in Washington, D.C., name it for them, and explain that this is an important clue. Tell them that the woman, Eddie Bernice Johnson, does a lot of her work in this government building, and that they are about to learn more about what she does.

Writing Tip:
Imitate a Model

Imitating written passages provides structure for students who are learning to write. Have them work in pairs to imitate the riddles presented in this chapter. Suggest that they focus on members of their own school community. Then ask volunteers to present their riddles for classmates to answer.

Transparency 4E

Transparency 4F

2 **Open the Big Book to Reading Further 4.** Read the text aloud while students follow along. Then revisit the text as you explain and discuss the following:

- From the introduction, we know that Eddie Bernice Johnson is a Texas woman in Congress. Help students understand that she is one of hundreds of people who work in the Capitol building in Washington, D.C. In our democracy, the people in all fifty states vote for their own Congresswomen and Congressmen. The leaders who are elected this way work to help the people of their state, just as Ms. Johnson works to help the people of Texas.

- You may want to use a U.S. wall map to point out the city of Dallas, the state of Texas, and the nation's capital, Washington, D.C., as they relate to Ms. Johnson's jobs and the people she helps. You may also want to locate your own city and state for students, explaining that your state, too, has people who work in Congress, doing jobs that will help the people in your state.

- Our leaders in Congress vote to make laws for the country, very much like a city council votes to make laws for the city. Remind the class about the process of voting on laws that they read about in Reading Further 3, "Let's Vote on It."

- Our leaders in Congress also vote to decide how to spend the country's money. Go through the text again with students, helping them find answers to the question, *What were some things that Ms. Johnson was willing to spend the country's money on?* (books for poor children, making a city a better place to live, helping her state in a natural disaster)

3 **Work with students to identify the different levels of government represented by public officials in this story.** Point out and discuss the visual symbols connected to the mayor (city hall seal), the governor (state outline), and the president (presidential seal with eagle). Again, you may want to refer to the wall map. Explain that these three leaders of a city, a state, and our country's government are all chosen by the people who vote; this is how a democracy works.

4 **Help students recognize that government jobs are service jobs.** Remind students what they read about the teacher, principal, school secretary, and custodian. Ask: *Why do we say that jobs in a school are service jobs?* Explain that like school workers, these government workers (Congresswoman, mayor, governor, and president) all have service jobs. In each case, ask: *What service does this person provide? Who are the people being helped?*

5 **Help the class identify the contributions of leaders at different levels of government.** Have students open their Interactive Student Notebooks to Reading Further 4. Point out how the information about three different government leaders is organized into a chart. Read the chart aloud as students follow along. Help them relate the visual symbols in the chart to the symbols they saw on the pages of the Big Book. In the symbol for state governor, help the students locate their state on the map and circle it or put a dot on it. Then read the riddles together and help students find the answers in the chart.

Processing

1   **Have student complete the Processing activity to synthesize what they have learned about the jobs of people at school.** Tell students they are going to create a class book. The book will include their own pictures showing how a teacher, principal, school secretary, and school custodian do their jobs.

Student Handouts 4C–4N

- Distribute *Student Handouts 4C–4N: Class Book.* There are twelve hand-outs, three per school helper; each student should receive one handout. Explain that they will each draw a picture for a class book about school helpers. Their handout will tell them which helper to draw.

- Before students begin work on their page, have them turn to Processing 4 in their Interactive Student Notebooks for some prewriting work. Read the directions aloud and encourage students to use this page to brain-storm ideas for their class book page. Be sure they understand they are to address just one aspect of the job: what their helper *sees, hears,* or *touches.*

- Allow students to turn to their handout to complete the class book page whenever they are ready.

2   **When students have completed their pages, compile them as a class book, *Who Helps Us at School?*** Consider having students collaborate on a special cover for their book.

Assessment

Masters for the chapter assessment appear in the *Lesson Masters.* Answers appear below.

Big Ideas

1. red circle: lower right picture

2. blue circle: upper right picture

3. green circle: lower left picture

4. brown circle: upper left picture

5. governor: state

   mayor: city

   president: country

   principal: school

Show You Know

6. Answers will vary. Drawings should show an adult helping children at school. Students should fill in the blank with a word from the Word Bank or another suitable word (e.g., nurse, librarian).

English Language Learners

For the interview and talking statue act-it-outs, help students participate by giving them a *scripted* act-it-out. As they come up to portray each of the school workers, provide them with cards that contain some basic vocabulary words in sentences that describe the worker's role at school. For example, "I am a teacher. I teach reading."

Students with Special Needs

After students listen to the CD tracks and make quick sketches of the service providers they will portray in each act-it-out, assist them in writing a caption for each picture. In this way, the learning will be reinforced through multiple modalities: drawing the picture, orally describing what they drew, and seeing in writing the words that explain the picture.

Enrichment

Have students complete a research project in which they ask parents or a librarian to help them find the name of:

- the mayor of their city
- the governor of their state
- the president of the country
- someone who works in Congress from their state

Ask students to enlist the help of adults or older siblings in finding Internet or newspaper pictures of these people, which can be made into a class display of "Our Leaders." Use this display to have students write "Who Am I?" riddles to present to their classmates. They might model their riddles on those in Reading Further 4 in the Interactive Student Notebook. The answers should be the proper names of the leaders shown in your class display.

Enrichment Resources

Have students find out more about service jobs by exploring the following Enrichment Resources for *Social Studies Alive! My School and Family,* at www.learntci.com.

Internet Connections

These recommended Web sites provide useful and engaging content that enforces skills development and mastery of subjects within the chapter.

Enrichment Readings

These in-depth readings encourage students to explore selected topics related to the chapter. For Chapter 4, you may wish to use one or more of the Enrichment Readings listed for the chapter. You may also find readings that relate the chapter's content directly to your state's curriculum.

Additional Reading Opportunities

The following books, which can be read aloud to students, offer opportunities to extend the content in this chapter.

The Frog Principal by Stephanie Calmenson. Illustrated by Denise Brunkus. (New York: Scholastic Press, 2001)

In a twist on the classic Frog Prince fairy tale, this picture book tells how the students of P.S. 88 rescue their principal from a visiting magician's accidental trick. This offers an amusing look at the principal's many roles.

If I Were President by Catherine Stier. Illustrated by DyAnne DiSalvo-Ryan. (Morton Grove, IL: Albert Whitman, 2004)

As children from diverse ethnic backgrounds take turns posing as the president of the United States, their day-to-day activities reveal the duties and rewards of the position in simple terms. This book offers a good introduction to the ways public servants help the people who elected them.

Try Your Best by Robert McKissack. Illustrated by Joe Cepeda. (New York: Harcourt School Publishers, 2004)

This easy-to-read book with simple dialogue is part of the Green Light Readers series. It tells the story of another school helper, the gym teacher Mr. York, who helps his students develop self-confidence by urging them to "try your best."

Choose a word to match each picture.

Word Bank			
Principal	Secretary	Custodian	Teacher

Teacher

Custodian

Secretary

Principal

Read each riddle. Who can help with
the problem? Draw a line to that person.

1. I am sick today.
   Who should Dad
   call at school?

2. My friend spilled
   her milk. Who can
   help clean it up?

3. My mom wants to know
   about school rules.
   Who should she ask?

4. I want to learn about
   animals. Who can
   help me?

1. When there are floods, I get help for the people

   in my state.

   I am the _____ *governor* _____ .

2. I am the leader of the United States.

   I am the _____ *president* _____ .

3. If your city streets need fixing, you can talk to me.

   I am the _____ *mayor* _____ .

How Are We Good Helpers at School?

Overview

Students discover that they can make valuable contributions at school by helping others, respecting school property, being positive, and solving problems. In the Preview activity, students think about ways they help at home. In Response Group activities, they explore four situations that they might encounter at school and discuss three options for each case before choosing the best way to be a good helper. In Reading Further, they learn about a historic figure who spent her life helping others. Finally, in a Processing activity, students create awards for people who have been good helpers at their school.

Objectives

Social Studies

- Make decisions about the best way to be a good citizen.
- List four characteristics of being a good citizen.
- Identify similarities and differences between life in the past and life in the present.

Language Arts

- Present reasons for a choice and persuade others. (speaking)
- Identify character traits from a nonfiction passage. (reading)

Social Studies Vocabulary

help others, take care of our things, do our best, respect others

Materials

Social Studies Alive! My School and Family Big Book and Student Editions

Transparencies 5A and 5B

Interactive Student Notebooks

Lesson Masters
- Information Masters 5A–5F
- Student Handout 5

CD Track 7

Time Estimates

Preview: 15 min.

Response Group: 3 sessions (varying lengths)

Reading Further: 30 min.

Processing: 30 min.

Activity	Suggested Time	Materials
Preview • Connecting to Prior Knowledge • Building Background Knowledge • Developing Vocabulary	15 minutes	• Interactive Student Notebooks
Response Group Making decisions about being good citizens in the classroom	*Phase 1* 30-minute session • Situation 1 (Steps 1–4) 45-minute session • Situations 2–4 (Step 5) *Phase 2* 30-minute session • Reading (Steps 6–11)	• Information Masters 5A–5D (1 transparency of each) • *Social Studies Alive! My School and Family* Big Book and Student Editions, Sections 5.1–5.4 • Transparency 5A (optional) • Interactive Student Notebooks • Information Master 5E (1 transparency) • CD Track 7
Reading Further Reading a historical biography	30 minutes	• *Social Studies Alive! My School and Family* Big Book, Chapter 5 Reading Further • Transparency 5B • Interactive Student Notebooks
Processing Honoring good citizens at school	30 minutes	• Interactive Student Notebooks • Information Master 5F (1 transparency) • Student Handout 5 (1 per student)
Assessment	15 minutes	• Chapter 5 Assessment, Lesson Masters • Chapter 5 Assessment, Digital Teacher Resources

Preview

1 **Connecting to Prior Knowledge:** Have students open their Interactive Student Notebooks to Preview 5.

- Read the directions and explain that students should think about ways they help out at home. They may write or draw their ideas.

- Encourage students to think beyond conventional tasks, such as taking out the trash and feeding pets. Suggest that they think of little things they do out of kindness—to be a help to the people who live with them.

- When students are ready to share, list their contributions on the board. Acknowledge that there are many ways students can be good helpers at home.

2 **Building Background Knowledge:** Put students into mixed-ability groups of three to practice making choices about being good helpers and good citizens.

- Give students the following question and three possible answers.

  Which of these answers is the best way to help out at home?

  (A) Pick up your toys without being told.

  (B) Ignore the adult who asks you to clean your room.

  (C) Set the table when someone asks you to.

- Tell students to discuss the question in their group, decide which is the best answer, and think about why they chose that answer.

- Ask students to justify their answers and explain why they did or did not choose answer B. Have them discuss why A and C are positive choices.

- Tell the class that in this lesson they will be presented with some situations and questions about how they can be good helpers at school.

3 **Developing Vocabulary:** Cover New Ideas—*help others, take care of our things, do our best,* and *respect others*—as they arise in the text. You may want to discuss some terms before beginning the activity, using methods described in *Solutions for Effective Instruction.*

Response Group

Phase 1: Making Decisions about Good Citizenship

1 **Introduce the Response Group guidelines.** Keep students in their mixed-ability groups of three. Read the following guidelines to help them understand how to work in Response Groups:

- Sit cross-legged.

- Sit with your knees touching the knees of others in your group.

- Give everyone a chance to talk.

- Listen to others when they talk.

- When your group has finished talking, straighten your legs out in front of you. This signals to the teacher that you are ready to share your ideas.

2 Introduce the first situation for which students consider how to be most helpful. Project *Information Master 5A: Situation 1: Spilled Crayons.* Follow these steps:

Information Master 5A

- Cover the text on the transparency. Ask: *What do you see in this picture? What do you think is happening?*

- Uncover the text and read it aloud. Help students identify which part describes the problem and which describes possible solutions.

- Review the three steps at the bottom of the transparency. For Step 2, emphasize that groups must pick the *best* choice, even though there may be more than one acceptable answer. For Step 3, remind students that act-it-outs are simple skits.

- Give groups about three minutes to discuss the answers and create their act-it-outs. If any group has trouble agreeing on an answer, suggest that they vote within their group and take the majority decision. Remind students to straighten their legs after they have decided on their act-it-outs. You may want to allow another minute or two for them to rehearse.

3 To demonstrate the results of their decision making, have groups perform their act-it-outs for the class. After each performance, ask the class to identify the group's answer.

- Have a Presenter from the group justify that answer. (**Note:** To save time, you may want to have only a few groups conduct their act-it-outs. Remind the other groups that they will have an opportunity to perform for the other situations. Have Presenters from those groups share their answers and reasoning.)

- After the last act-it-out for Situation 1, ask: *Which answers did groups choose?* (A or C) *Why is B not a good choice?*

4 Invite groups to persuade others to agree with their decision. Have groups kneel facing each other. Tell the A teams they will have two minutes to try to convince members of the C teams to change their minds. Call on volunteers from the A teams to justify why A is the best answer. Allow students from the C teams to cross over to the A teams if they find the arguments convincing. Similarly, allow the C teams to try to convince members of the A teams to change their minds.

5 Repeat Steps 2–4 for the next three decision-making situations. Remind students to follow the Response Group guidelines. For each situation, ask: *What is the problem? What are the possible solutions?*

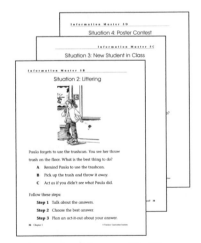

Information Masters 5B–5D

- Project *Information Master 5B: Situation 2: Littering.* After groups perform their act-it-outs and justify their choice of answer, ask: *Which answers did groups choose?* (A or B) *Why is C not a good choice?* Have teams A and B alternate as they try to convince the other students that their answer is better.

- Project *Information Master 5C: Situation 3: New Student in Class.* Follow the same procedures. After the act-it-outs, ask: *Which answers did groups choose?* (B or C) *Why is A not a good choice?* Allow teams B and C to try persuading each other to change sides.

- Project *Information Master 5D: Situation 4: Poster Contest.* After the act-it-outs, ask: *Which answers did groups choose?* (A or B) *Why is C not a good choice?* Again, allow teams A and B to face off and argue for their answer as the better choice.

Phase 2: Learning More About Ways We Help at School

6 **To give an overview of the characteristics of a good citizen at school, introduce the "Good Helpers" song.** Project a transparency of *Information Master 5E: "Good Helpers"* while you play the song on CD Track 7. Help students follow the lyrics as they listen to the song. Then sing the song together until students are comfortable with the lyrics.

7 **Introduce the New Ideas.** Use the introduction to Chapter 5 in the Big Book or project *Transparency 5A: How Are We Good Helpers at School?* to review the New Ideas: *help others, take care of our things* (respect property), *do our best* (take initiative), and *respect others* (have a good attitude). Ask:

- What do you see in this picture?

- Where might this be happening?

- What different things are happening?

- How are the different children being good helpers at school?

8 **Turn through Sections 5.1–5.4 in the Big Book, reading aloud just the headings.** On each page, ask students to look carefully at the pictures and identify who is being a good helper and how.

9 **Have students learn about being good helpers by reading Section 5.1 of the Student Edition.** Read the section aloud as students follow along. Help them brainstorm answers to the question at the end of the page.

10 **To review what students have learned about being good helpers, have them open their Interactive Student Notebooks to Reading Notes 5.** Model how to complete the first page of notes, telling students they should list two things that they can do to help others and draw one of them. Encourage them to use sentences in the Student Edition as models for their writing. If they want to write their own ideas, offer spelling help as needed.

11 **Repeat Steps 9 and 10 for Sections 5.2–5.4 in the Student Edition.**

Information Master 5E

Transparency 5A

Vocabulary Development: Develop Concepts

Brainstorm with the class some characteristics of respect. On chart paper, create a three-column chart to record what respect looks like, sounds like, and feels like. Write students' ideas in the chart. Add to this chart over time as you see respectful behavior in the classroom.

Reading Further: Clara Barton Helped Others

1 **Project *Transparency 5B: Clara Barton.*** Ask the following visual discovery questions to help students analyze the image and make some predictions.

Transparency 5B

- What do you see in this picture?

- What does the woman seem to be doing?

- What do you see behind the woman and man?

- If you were in this scene, what might you hear?

- Where do you think these people might be?

- Do you think this is a picture of something you might see today? Why or why not?

2 **Tell students that this is a picture of Clara Barton, a famous woman in our country's history.** Ask: *Who knows what we mean by the word* history? Help students understand that history is the story of things that happened long ago and of people who lived long ago.

- Write *past* and *present* on the board. Ask: *Which word would we use to mean things that happened long ago? Which word means things that are happening now?* Explain that we can read history books and look at old photographs to learn about the past, while we might watch the news on TV to learn about the present.

3 **Help students explore the ways Clara Barton was a good helper and a good citizen.** Ask them to follow along while you read aloud the Reading Further from the Big Book. After reading, help students reflect on what made Clara Barton a good helper. Ask:

- What did you learn about Clara Barton? What words could you use to describe her?

- What was her first job? Whom did she treat with respect?

- What did she do during the war? In what way was she brave?

4 **Have students open their Interactive Student Notebooks to Reading Further 5.** Work through Part A as a class, identifying three ways Clara Barton helped people.

- Read aloud the directions for Part A. Call on volunteers to tell something they remember from the story about how Clara Barton helped people long ago. As they give their ideas, write a word bank on the board.

- Next, read the directions for Part B. Help students find the story in their Student Edition. Have pairs talk together about what clues in the images show that life long ago was different, in some ways, from life today. Have them work individually to draw their own pictures showing something about life in Clara Barton's day.

> **Reading Strategy: Make and Check Predictions**
>
> Before reading the Clara Barton story, have students look at the image on each page. Ask them what they think they will learn about the ways in which Clara Barton was a good helper. List their ideas on the board. After reading the story aloud, review the listed ideas and ask students which ones were right. Put a check by each correct prediction.

- Finally, read aloud the directions for Part C. Help students understand that even though some parts of life in the past were different from today, people who lived long ago did some of the same things that people still do today. Encourage students to think of themselves as helpers working with a modern-day Clara Barton. Have them think about how they could work with Clara to be good helpers today.

- Ask for a few volunteers to share and describe their drawings.

Processing

1   **Have students demonstrate that they recognize good citizenship in the school setting by completing the Processing activity.** Project a transparency of *Information Master 5F: Making a Helping Hand Award.* Read it aloud as students follow along. Explain that a Helping Hand Award honors school helpers who help others, take care of things, do their best, and respect others. Explain that students will make a Helping Hand Award for a person they know at their school. The person can be an adult or another student.

2   **Distribute a copy of *Student Handout 5: Helping Hand Award* to each student.** For pre-writing work, have students open their Interactive Student Notebooks to Processing 5. Explain that this is a brainstorming page they will use as they think about who deserves a Helping Hand Award.

   - As a class, brainstorm names of people to honor with a Helping Hand Award. Record students' nominations on the board. Tell them to write the ideas they like best in their Interactive Student Notebooks.

   - As a class, brainstorm ways to decorate a Helping Hand Award. Have students sketch the ideas they like best on their brainstorming page.

   - Leave Information Master 5F posted for reference as students create their awards. Be sure they understand that the helper's name goes in the top banner, and the reason for the award goes in the box above the picture they will draw.

3   **Have students conduct an "awards ceremony" celebrating the people who make a difference at school.**

Information Master 5F

Student Handout 5

Assessment

Masters for the chapter assessment appear in the *Lesson Masters.* Answers appear below.

Big Ideas

1. circle: the two children sitting at the computer

2. color blue: the books being picked up by the girl

3. She started the American Red Cross.

Show You Know

4. Answers will vary. Sample answer: Say thank you. The drawing should match the student's written idea.

English Language Learners

For the Processing assignment, provide students with a word bank containing relevant terms from the lesson and other concepts they can use to create their awards. For example, you might include words such as *helper, school, respect, care, recess, playground, crossing guard, parent, field trip driver,* and so forth.

Students with Special Needs

For the topics discussed on each page in the Student Edition, ask students to do a mini act-it-out or role-play for the rest of the class. For example:

- Section 5.1, We Help Others: Leave some materials on a desk and ask students to model cleaning up.

- Section 5.2, We Take Care of Our Things: Leave out a ball from recess and ask students to model putting it away.

- Section 5.3, We Do Our Best: Ask students to demonstrate how to line up quickly and quietly for recess.

- Section 5.4, We Respect Others: Have students model an appropriate way to say "please" and "thank you."

These demonstrations will reinforce concepts for participating students, as they see and hear ideas in the text and then physically model them. Those observing the act-it-outs also benefit from seeing the concepts modeled by their peers.

Enrichment

For additional decision-making practice that requires students to suggest their own solutions, form small groups and present this situation: *A team of four children is sitting at the art table. The teacher has asked them to work together to create a poster about Clara Barton. One person on the team is daydreaming and drawing a picture of dragons. What's the best thing to do?* Tell each group to think of three possible ways to respond. Call on groups to perform act-it-outs demonstrating different responses. Student volunteers can then lead the class in the discussion of which responses are appropriate, which are not appropriate, and why they aren't appropriate.

You may also wish to extend the Processing activity for use with class read-alouds. Have students make and present Helping Hand Awards for a helpful character in a book—either a real person such as Clara Barton or a fictional person such as the woodcutter in *Little Red Riding Hood*. Discuss with students the clues in a story that tell us whether someone is a real person or a make-believe character. Have them add the label *Real* or *Make-believe* to their book-character Helping Hand Awards.

Enrichment Resources

Have students find out more about the contributions of good citizens by exploring the following Enrichment Resources for *Social Studies Alive! My School and Family* at www.learntci.com.

Internet Connections

These recommended Web sites provide useful and engaging content that enforces skills development and mastery of subjects within the chapter.

Enrichment Readings

These in-depth readings encourage students to explore selected topics related to the chapter. For Chapter 5, you may wish to use one or more of the Enrichment Readings listed for the chapter. You may also find readings that relate the chapter's content directly to your state's curriculum.

Additional Reading Opportunities

The following fiction and nonfiction books, which can be read aloud to students, offer opportunities to extend the content in this chapter.

The Biggest and Brightest Light: A True Story of the Heart by Marilyn Perlyn. Illustrated by Amanda Perlyn. (San Francisco: Robert D. Reed Publishers, 2004)

This true story describes how a first-grade girl responds to her teacher's anguish when she reveals that her daughter is very sick. It demonstrates that even the smallest acts of kindness and thoughtfulness can have a lifetime impact, and reinforces the concept that no one is too young to help others.

How Do Dinosaurs Go to School? by Jane Yolen. Illustrated by Mark Teague. (New York: Scholastic, The Blue Sky Press, 2007)

Do dinosaurs push or talk too loudly in school, or do they behave as good children do? With colorful illustrations of dinosaurs in school situations, this book takes a humorous look at how students can behave like good citizens in the classroom.

The New Kid by Susan Hood. Photographs by Dorothy Handelman. (Brookfield, CT: Millbrook Press, 1998)

What happens when a new child arrives in class? It can be disruptive, until one child remembers how it feels to be "the new kid" and befriends him. Photographs and a phonics-based text make this an easy-to-read book about being a good citizen in the classroom.

List two ways you help others at school.

Answers may vary. Possible answers:

1. We help the teacher clean up.

2. We share books with friends.

Draw one way you help others at school.

Drawings will vary.

List two ways you take care of your things at school.

Answers may vary. Possible answers:

1. We are careful with our crayons.

2. We put our balls away after recess.

Draw one way you take care of your things at school.

Drawings will vary.

List two ways you do your best at school.

Answers may vary. Possible answers:

1. We ask questions.

2. We line up for recess.

Draw one way you do your best at school.

Drawings will vary.

List two ways you respect others at school.

Answers may vary. Possible answers:

1. We say "please" and "thank you."

2. We are good winners and losers.

Draw one way you respect others at school.

Drawings will vary.

Part A

Clara Barton lived long ago. She lived by the Golden Rule. List three things that Clara did to help people.

1. Clara was a teacher. She helped children learn.

2. Clara was a nurse. She helped men who were hurt.

3. Clara started the American Red Cross. It helps people in need.

Part B

Look at the pictures of Clara Barton in your book. What is one way that life in the past was different? Draw or write your answer.

Answers will vary.

What Is a Map?

Overview

Students learn what maps are and how to use them. In the Preview, they listen to a story about an escaped mouse and then help create a 3-D map of the classroom in which the story is set. In a Social Studies Skill Builder, they practice reading a map of the same classroom. Reading Further gives an overview of several other types of maps, and students discuss what each one shows. Finally, in a Processing activity, students use what they have learned to create a simple map of their own.

Objectives

Social Studies

- Create a three-dimensional setting that corresponds to a two-dimensional map.
- Read a classroom map.
- Use a compass rose to determine direction.
- Identify maps that show local areas, the United States, and the world.
- Use symbols to create a classroom map.

Language Arts

- Retell a story in sequence. (listening and speaking)

Social Studies Vocabulary

map, symbol, map key, compass rose, direction

Materials

Social Studies Alive! My School and Family Big Book and Student Editions

Transparencies 6A–6C

Placards 6A–6H

Interactive Student Notebooks

Lesson Masters
- Information Master 6
- Student Handout 6

Interactive Desk Maps

Time Estimates

Preview: 30 min.

Social Studies Skill Builder: 3 sessions (varying lengths)

Reading Further: 30 min.

Processing: 30 min.

Activity	Suggested Time	Materials
Preview • Connecting to Prior Knowledge • Developing Vocabulary • Building Background Knowledge	30 minutes	• Transparency 6A • Placards 6A–6H • Interactive Student Notebooks
Social Studies Skill Builder Exploring maps, map keys, and the cardinal directions	*Phase 1* 30-minute session • Relating objects to map symbols (Steps 1–3) *Phase 2* 50-minute sessions (2) • Using a map (Steps 4–6) • Reading about map features (Steps 7–11)	• Transparency 6A • Placards 6A–6H • *Social Studies Alive! My School and Family* Big Book and Student Editions, Sections 6.1–6.4 • Transparency 6B • Interactive Student Notebooks
Reading Further Comparing what can be found on maps of a school, a community, a state, a country, and the world	30 minutes	• *Social Studies Alive! My School and Family* Big Book, Chapter 6 Reading Further • Transparency 6C • Interactive Student Notebooks • Interactive Desk Maps • map of your state (optional)
Processing Creating a new classroom map	30 minutes	• Interactive Student Notebooks • Student Handout 6 (1 per student)
Assessment		• Chapter 6 Assessment, Lesson Masters • Chapter 6 Assessment, Digital Teacher Resources

Preview

1   Connecting to Prior Knowledge: Help students think about what they already know about maps.

- Have students open their Interactive Student Notebooks to Preview 6. Tell them that these two pictures show different kinds of maps they may have seen. If they have an idea about what a particular map shows, they should write their idea below that map.

- When students are done, ask volunteers to share their ideas about what these maps show (*a map of a zoo, and an area road map*).

2   Developing Vocabulary: Cover New Ideas—*map, symbol, map key, compass rose,* and *direction*—as they arise in the text. You may want to discuss some terms before beginning the activity, using methods described in *Solutions for Effective Instruction.*

3   Building Background Knowledge: Prepare students for this mapping lesson by reading them the story *Yikes! A Mouse!* After hearing the story, students will re-create the scene in their own classroom.

- Gather the class in a reading circle while you project *Transparency 6A: What Is a Map?* Tell students that this is a picture of Ms. Hutchinson's first grade class. Let them know that you are going to read a story about one special day in Ms. Hutchinson's classroom. Read aloud the story on *Information Master 6: Yikes! A Mouse!* Omit the last paragraph.

- Ask students to retrace the teacher's steps and name the objects she passed as she looked for the mouse. Point to each object on the transparency as students name it: door, round tables, cabinet, teacher's desk, student desks, recess basket, rectangular table, and computer.

- Place *Placards 6A–6H: Classroom Objects* in random order on the chalk rail. Ask students to identify each picture.

- Prepare to re-create the story. Consult the classroom map on Transparency 6B to see how the room is laid out. Clear a space in your room in which to re-create the map.

- Tell the class you will read the story again. This time, they will use the placards to re-create the setting of the story. Explain that you will stop reading each time a new object is mentioned.

- Each time you pause for a new object, ask a volunteer to come to the front of the classroom, find the placard for that object, and stand in an assigned location that roughly correlates with that of the object on the map. (**Note:** Double up as necessary to give each student a role. There are eight placards plus two acting roles, the Teacher and the Mouse. With a large class, you might duplicate Placards 6B and 6F in order to have students representing both round tables and all twelve student desks.)

Transparency 6A

Information Master 6

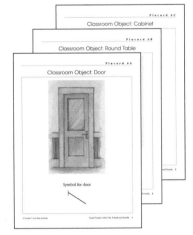

Placards 6A–6H

- At the end of the story, call attention to the image on the transparency. Help students to see that they are now standing in roughly the positions of the objects in that scene.

- Choose a Teacher and a Mouse for a third telling of the story. Encourage students to retell the story themselves, but provide help if they get stuck. As the Teacher walks the route taken by Ms. Hutchinson, have the class say the name of each object she passes. When the teacher gets to the computer, the "mouse" can squeak. After the mouse squeaks, have all the students say in unison, "Yikes! A mouse!" Let students know that they will hear and re-create the story again tomorrow.

Social Studies Skill Builder

Phase 1: Create a 3-D Model of a Map with Pictures of a Location

1 **Gather students in their reading circle to revisit the classroom that they will see mapped in this lesson.** Project Transparency 6A again and reread the story *Yikes! A Mouse!* on Information Master 6. This time, include the last paragraph of the story.

2 **Distribute Placards 6A–6H to re-create the classroom shown in the map.**

- Have students stand in their locations from the day before. Remind them that they are standing in the positions of the objects in the classroom scene on the transparency.

- Ask students to look at the small picture at the bottom of their cards. Explain that this is a symbol of the object pictured on the card, and that a symbol is a simple drawing that stands for a bigger idea. These symbols of things in the classroom will help students see the classroom the way the mouse saw it from the ceiling.

3 **With students' help, draw a map of Ms. Hutchinson's classroom on the board.** Don't let students know what you are drawing until the map is complete.

- Draw a large rectangle on the board to represent Ms. Hutchinson's four classroom walls.

- Ask each placard holder to come to the front of the room, one at a time, and say the name of the object on the placard. Draw the symbol of that object in the correct location on your map. Remember to draw two round table symbols and twelve student desk symbols. The placard holder can place the placard on the chalk rail and sit down after you draw the symbol or symbols.

- When you have drawn all the symbols on the board, ask students if they know what you have drawn. Explain that you have created a map of Ms. Hutchinson's classroom.

Speaking and Listening: Choral Reading

Write on the board, "No white mouse." During this third telling of the story, point to the phrase at appropriate times and ask students to chime in on the repeated phrase, "No white mouse."

Phase 2: Read a Map Using Symbols and the Compass Rose

4 **Discuss the basic features of a map.** Turn to Chapter 6 in the *Social Studies Alive! My School and Family* Big Book. Introduce the New Ideas (*map, symbol, map key, compass rose,* and *direction*) by reading aloud the headings of Sections 6.1–6.4. Encourage students to look carefully at the pictures and answer these questions:

- For Section 6.1: *What place does this map show?*

- For Section 6.2: *Where do you see these symbols in the map on the opposite page? What do you think they stand for?*

- For Section 6.3: *What do you see in the map key? Who can show me one symbol in the key and locate the same symbol on the map?*

- For Section 6.4: *This symbol, called a compass rose, has four letters that stand for four directions. What letters do you see? The letter N stands for north. You can see that north points up. What is something you see on the north side of the map on the opposite page?*

5 **Explain that students are about to practice reading a map.** Place students in mixed-ability pairs. Have them open their *Social Studies Alive! My School and Family* Student Editions to Section 6.3, where they will see a map with a key. Remind students that this is a map of Ms. Hutchinson's classroom. Tell them you will read some directions, and they should use one finger to follow these directions on their map. Let students know they should help their partners throughout the activity.

6 **Guide students in reading the classroom map.** Project *Transparency 6B: Map of Ms. Hutchinson's Classroom,* and read the directions below. Demonstrate following each direction after students have had a chance to try it themselves.

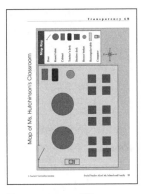

Transparency 6B

- Run your finger around the four walls of Ms. Hutchinson's classroom.

- Run your finger around the map key.

- Count the number of symbols on the map key. How many are there? *(eight)*

- Find the door on the map. Touch the door with your finger.

- Touch the round tables.

- Touch the computer.

- Touch the rectangular table.

- Touch the student desks. Count them. How many are there? *(twelve)*

- Touch the recess basket.

- Point to the part of the map that shows directions.

- Touch the N. N means north. Touch the north wall of Ms. Hutchinson's classroom.

- Put your finger on the S. S means south. Touch the south wall.

- Put your finger on the W. W means west. Touch the west wall.

- E means east. Put your finger on the E. Touch the east wall of the classroom.

7 **Review the term *map*.** Read aloud Section 6.1 in the Student Edition as students follow along in their books. Then ask for volunteers to share another kind of map they have seen and to tell what it shows.

8 **Read about map symbols.** Read aloud Section 6.2 as students follow along. Explain that we can draw a symbol for anything. We often use simple shapes for symbols. Suggest objects in your own classroom, and ask volunteers to share their ideas for a symbol for each object. Allow them to draw their symbols on the board.

9 **Read about a map key.** Read aloud Section 6.3 as students follow along. Then ask volunteers to identify different symbols on the map.

10 **Read about the four cardinal directions.** Read aloud Section 6.4 as students follow along. Then ask volunteers to share a direction they know.

- Write *north, south, east,* and *west* on the board at the ends of crossed arrows pointing up and down, right and left. Explain that these directions can help you find places on a map and also in the real world.

- Locate north in your classroom. Have students stand up and face north, with their arms extended to the each side at shoulder height. Explain that when they are facing north, their left hand points west, and their right hand points east. Help them relate this to the arrows that point left and right on a map's compass rose. Ask a volunteer to stand up and walk toward the north, south, east, or west.

- For further work on the cardinal directions, project Transparency 6B again. Have students locate the part of this map that shows that north is up (the compass rose). Then ask questions like these: *What is south of the two round tables? Is the computer on the east side or the west side of the room? If you were standing by the computer, what direction would you walk to get to the classroom door? Is the recess basket north or south of the teacher's desk?*

11 **Have students demonstrate their understanding of map symbols by completing Reading Notes 6 in their Interactive Student Notebooks.** Be sure students understand that they should color each symbol, both in the key and on the map. Read the directions aloud as students color the map of Ms. Hutchinson's classroom.

Vocabulary Development: Use Directional Words

In addition to the cardinal directions, help students recognize and use four terms for relative or personal directions. Write on the board *left, right, front, back*. Ask students to face the front of the classroom. As you designate particular points in the room, have students call out which direction they would go to reach that point.

Reading Further: The Right Kind of Map

Transparency 6C

1 **Project** *Transparency 6C: A School Map.*

   - Ask questions such as: *What do you see? What clues are there that this is a map? What kind of place do you think this map shows? What makes you think so? Who might use this kind of map?*

   - Explain to students that you are going to read a story that tells about some children who use this map as they go on a special kind of treasure hunt. (**Note:** Keep the transparency at hand so that students can trace the children's trail through their school.)

2 **Open the Big Book to Reading Further 6.** Read aloud the first two pages as students follow along in their Student Editions. Help students identify the point of view by asking: *Who do you think is telling this story?*

3 **Give students a chance to practice reading the school map.**

   - Help students identify the different regions of the school that are shown on the map: the office area, the playground, the library and computer lab, the multi-use room, the restrooms, and the classrooms. Where possible, relate these to areas of your school that students are familiar with. Ask: *How do you know where one region ends and the next one begins? How are these boundaries shown on the school map?*

   - Point to Mr. Kelly's room and ask: *Which is nearer to Mr. Kelly's room, the library or the computer lab? Starting at Mr. Kelly's room, which direction will the children walk to get to the library?* Help students use the directions on the compass to decide that the children walk south to get to the library. Have a volunteer trace their path on the school map on the transparency.

4 **Introduce the globe and world map by reading aloud page 60 in the Big Book as students follow along.**

   - Ask: *What can you see on a globe? How is a globe the same as the world map? How is it different? How can we tell which areas are land and which are water? Where do people live?*

   - Point out and name the seven continents on the world map, explaining that the large areas of land where people live are called the *continents.* Point to North America and tell students that this is the continent where they live.

   - Ask volunteers to point to the oceans to the east, north, and west of our continent, North America. Name each ocean that students locate.

   - Briefly discuss the differences in scale. Students should see that on a globe, the continents are just inches wide, and on the playground map, they are just a few feet wide. In the real world, continents are many, many miles across. World maps show an enormously large area in a small space.

   - Just before reading the next page, have students look again at the school map on Transparency 6C and trace the path from Mr. Kelly's room to the library, to the playground, and then back inside the school to Mrs. Wong's room, where the children will be going next.

5   **Introduce the United States map by giving each student or pair of students an Interactive Desk Map.** Have them place the United States map face up. Then read aloud page 61 in the Big Book as students follow along. Show students how to locate their own state on the Interactive Desk Map. Ask: *Is our state nearer to the Atlantic or the Pacific Ocean? Are any states larger than ours? Smaller? Which part of the United States do we live in—are we farther north or south? Farther east or west?* (**Note:** The other side of the Interactive Desk Map, which shows a community map, will be used with a later chapter.)

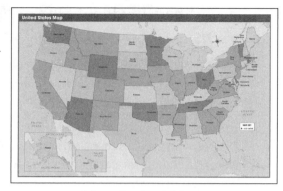

Interactive Desk Map

6   **Introduce the individual state map to students.** Read aloud page 62 in the Big Book as students follow along.

   • Read the map key aloud and have students find examples of each symbol on the map. Point out the Snake River and ask: *Is this river on the east side or west side of Oregon? What is located to the west of the state?*

   • Display a map of your own state, if available, and show students how to locate their community. Point out natural features of your state such as lakes, rivers, and mountains.

7   **Introduce the community map to students.** Read aloud page 63 in the Big Book.

   • Have students locate the school and the ice rink. Ask: *Which direction will Mr. Kelly's class go to get from the school to the ice rink? Which street will they go down?*

   • Have students compare distances on this map, using the terms *near* and *far*. Ask, for example: *Which is nearer to the school, the ice rink or the City Park? The hospital or the library?*

   • Tell students that every object on a community map like this one has a street address, with a particular number. Give the address of your school as an example. Ask volunteers to give their home address. (**Note:** An address like this indicates *absolute* location.)

   • Again call attention to Transparency 6C and have students find the location where the children in the story found "the right map." *(the office)* Call on a volunteer to retrace the children's route: from Mr. Kelly's class to the library, to the playground, to Mrs. Wong's room, to the computer lab, to the office.

8   **Have students open their Interactive Student Notebooks to Reading Further 6.** Read aloud the map riddles. Have students match each riddle with one of the maps shown on the opposite page. Help them fill in the blanks with words that name the appropriate map: school, town, United States, or world.

Processing

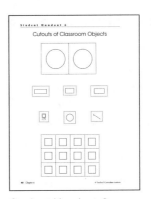

Student Handout 6

1   **Have students create a new classroom map as they complete Processing 6 in their Interactive Student Notebooks.** Distribute copies of *Student Handout 6: Cutouts of Classroom Objects*. Make available scissors and glue sticks. Then read aloud the directions on Processing 6. Explain that students will use the blank map space and cutouts from the handout to create a new classroom map. Emphasize that you want to see maps that are different from Ms. Hutchinson's classroom. Be sure students understand that the map they make might be quite different from the maps their neighbors make. Suggest that students could use ideas from their own classroom as they place the symbols on their map, or they could make up an all-new classroom.

2   **Have students share their maps and review the cardinal directions.** Gather the class in a large circle on the floor. One by one, have students hold up their new maps and explain why they arranged the objects the way they did. You can quiz them about the placement of certain objects, challenging them with questions that require the use of direction words in their answers. For example: *Where did you put the door? Where is the computer? Touch the north wall of the classroom on your map.*

Assessment

Masters for the chapter assessment appear in the *Lesson Masters*. Answers appear below.

Big Ideas

1. a place

2. South

3. town map

Show You Know

4. The bulleted points can serve as a rubric for this item.

English Language Learners

Have students make picture dictionaries for the social studies vocabulary and other map-related words from this lesson. They might include these terms: *map, symbol, map key, direction, compass rose, door, table, desk, cabinet, basket, computer, circle, round, rectangle.* Have them make each page look similar to Placards 6A–6H, with a simple picture and the related word. Students can color or draw their own pictures and copy (or trace) the terms from a placard or from the Student Edition. Bind each picture dictionary with staples or rings for the student's reference throughout the lesson.

Students with Special Needs

As students identify the elements of Ms. Hutchinson's classroom, have them also identify the location of a similar item in their own classroom. For example, when the term *computer* comes up during the first retelling of *Yikes! A Mouse!*, have students not only re-create the computer location in the fictional classroom but also point out the computer in your classroom. Repeat this process for the other items, such as door, table, and desk, so that the abstract map symbols have a link to something more concrete.

Enrichment

While the rest of the class works with Ms. Hutchinson's classroom during Phase 2, have a small group of students work together to create simple maps of their own classroom, similar to Ms. Hutchinson's. Ask them to make up five directions for others to follow as they look at these classroom maps. For example: *Point to the teacher's desk. Find the reading rug.* Later, during the Processing assignment, these students can apply what they know about maps by creating their "ideal" classroom.

Alternatively, have students create a 3-D model of their classroom or the school as a whole. They might use clay or cardboard to indicate the location of walls for each room or building. Small toy figures could be placed in the model to represent key people in the school.

Enrichment Resources

Have students find out more about maps by exploring the following Enrichment Resources for *Social Studies Alive! My School and Family* at www.learntci.com.

Internet Connections

These recommended Web sites provide useful and engaging content that enforces skills development and mastery of subjects within the chapter.

Enrichment Readings

These in-depth readings encourage students to explore selected topics related to the chapter. For Chapter 6, you may wish to use one or more of the Enrichment Readings listed for the chapter. You may also find readings that relate the chapter's content directy to your state's curriculum.

Additional Reading Opportunities

These books, which can be read aloud to students, offer opportunities to extend the content in this chapter.

Mapping Penny's World by Loreen Leedy (New York: Henry Holt, 2003)

Lisa sets out to make a map of the world that's familiar to her dog, Penny: Lisa's room, the yard, the neighborhood, and the nearby park, complete with trails. Students will see how maps reflect their daily lives.

Me on the Map by Joan Sweeney. Illustrated by Annette Cable. (New York: Dragonfly Books, 1998)

This book helps young students make sense of the abstraction of maps as a symbolic model of their own environment. It starts with floor plans of a girl's room and house and then expands from home to street, to town, to state, to country, and to the world.

There's a Map on My Lap! All About Maps by Tish Rabe. Illustrated by Aristides Ruiz. (New York: Random House Children's Books, 2002)

The Cat in the Hat teaches the young reader about maps and how to use them. Told in rhyme, this book provides an introduction to map-making: grids, compasses, topographical maps, scale, globes, atlases, and more.

Color the map.

Follow these steps:

1. Draw a brown line around the classroom.

2. Color the door orange.

3. Color the round tables green.

4. Color the cabinet orange.

5. Color the teacher's desk brown.

6. Color the student desks blue.

7. Color the recess basket yellow.

8. Color the computer black.

9. Color the rectangular table red.

10. Color the symbols in the map key to match your map.

Map of Ms. Hutchinson's Classroom

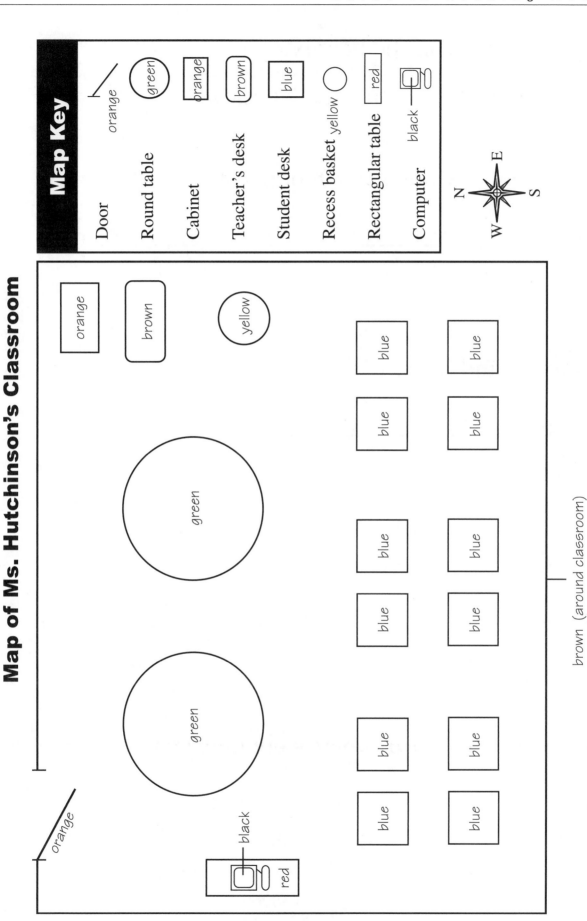

Map Key

Door	orange
Round table	green
Cabinet	orange
Teacher's desk	brown
Student desk	blue
Recess basket	yellow
Rectangular table	red
Computer	black

Look at the maps on the next page.

Choose words to fill in the blanks below.

1. I want to find what is north of my state.

   I need a _____ United States _____ map.

2. I want to find the school nurse's office.

   I need a _____ school _____ map.

3. I want to find City Hall.

   I need a _____ town _____ map.

4. I want to find Africa, where elephants live.

   I need a _____ world _____ map.

What Was School Like Long Ago?

Overview

Students compare schools of long ago to schools of today. In the Preview, they consider what "the past" means to them and learn that a time capsule can offer a glimpse into the past. In a Response Group activity, they view and read about school-related objects from the past, discussing their use. In Reading Further, students take a look at modes of transportation from times past. An elderly man's reminiscence about changes in modes of transportation over his lifetime serves as a model for students, as they construct a timeline of their own lives. In the Processing activity, students turn their attention from past to future as they predict and draw something that a school of the future might have.

Objectives

Social Studies

- Predict uses of pictured historical artifacts.
- Compare and contrast past and present community life, with an emphasis on schooling, children's lives, and transportation.
- Sequence a series of life events along a simple timeline.

Language Arts

- Make a brief presentation summarizing a small-group discussion. (speaking and listening)
- Organize time-related terms in sequence. (reading)

Social Studies Vocabulary

long ago, schoolhouse, hornbook

Materials

Social Studies Alive! My School and Family Big Book and Student Editions

Transparencies 7A–7I

Interactive Student Notebooks

Lesson Masters

- Student Handout 7

Time Estimates

Preview: 30 min.

Response Group: 4 sessions (35 min. each)

Reading Further: 45 min.

Processing: 40 min.

Activity	Suggested Time	Materials
Preview • Connecting to Prior Knowledge • Building Background Knowledge • Developing Vocabulary	30 minutes	• Transparencies 7A and 7B • Interactive Student Notebooks
Response Group Examining artifacts that represent school life in the past	*Phase 1* 35-minute sessions (2) • Examining artifacts (Steps 1–5) • Reading (Steps 6–8) *Phase 2* 35-minute sessions (2) • Examining artifacts (Steps 9–12) • Reading (Steps 13 and 14)	• *Social Studies Alive! My School and Family* Big Book and Student Editions, Sections 7.1 and 7.2 • Transparencies 7C–7E • Interactive Student Notebooks • *Social Studies Alive! My School and Family* Big Book and Student Editions, Sections 7.3 and 7.4 • Transparencies 7F–7H • Interactive Student Notebooks
Reading Further Observing changes in transportation over a lifetime of nearly 100 years	45 minutes	• *Social Studies Alive! My School and Family* Big Book and Student Editions, Chapter 7 Reading Further • Transparency 7I • Interactive Student Notebooks • Student Handout 7 (1 per student)
Processing Predicting one way schools will change in the future	40 minutes	• Interactive Student Notebooks
Assessment	15 minutes	• Chapter 7 Assessment, Lesson Masters • Chapter 7 Assessment, Digital Teacher Resources

Preview

1   **Connecting to Prior Knowledge:** Have students open their Interactive Student Notebooks to Preview 7.

Transparency 7A

- Read aloud the directions. Talk briefly about the pictured calendar, asking how a calendar shows months, weeks, and days. Compare this with your classroom calendar.

- Briefly discuss the term *past*. Ask students for a few ideas about what the past means to them. Then have students draw something that they think of when they think about the past. Ask a few volunteers to tell and show what they drew.

- Project *Transparency 7A: What Was School Like Long Ago?* Ask students to describe the setting they see. Tell them that this picture is set in a school from the past, more than 100 years ago. Ask them to find clues in the picture that tell us this is a scene from long ago. For example, they may mention the children's clothing, the stove, and the quill pen.

2   **Building Background Knowledge:** Introduce the idea of a time capsule by projecting *Transparency 7B: Time Capsule*.

Transparency 7B

- Ask students whether this box looks old or new. Explain that it was found buried in a schoolyard.

- Identify the box as a time capsule. Explain the following: People put everyday objects into a time capsule. Then they bury it where someone will find it many years later, in the future. When we find a time capsule, open it, and look at the things inside, we can learn something about what life was like for the people who buried it. Even though we might have to make some guesses about what we find, these things give us a very real picture of one part of life in the past.

- Tell students that this time capsule was buried in a schoolyard more than 100 years ago. Have them predict what could be inside the time capsule. Encourage them to think about objects they see in their own classroom as they discuss the possibilities.

3   **Developing Vocabulary:** Cover New Ideas—*long ago, schoolhouse,* and *hornbook*—as they arise in the text. You may want to discuss some terms before beginning the activity, using methods described in *Solutions for Effective Instruction*.

Response Groups

Phase 1: Examining Artifacts of Schools and Classrooms in the Past

1   **Remind students of the Response Group guidelines.** Put students in mixed-ability groups of three and name one student in each group to be the Presenter. Read the Response Group guidelines aloud:

   - Sit cross-legged with knees touching.

   - Give everyone a chance to talk.

   - Listen to others when they talk.

   - When the group is done talking, straighten your legs out in front of you.

2   **Project *Transparency 7C: Things at School: Object 1,* and ask students to predict what the artifact was used for.** Say that this is an object from long ago, but do not reveal what it is. Ask students to talk in their groups about what the object is and how it might have been used. When they have completed their discussions, ask each Presenter to share their group's ideas.

3   **Help students compare and contrast Object 1 to objects in schools today.** Identify the object as a coal-burning stove. Explain that long ago, schools had a stove similar to this to heat the classroom. Teachers had to keep putting more coal or wood into the stove to keep it going, especially during a cold winter. Older boys would help the teacher bring in the heavy coal or the wood from outside. Ask: *How is this different from schools today?*

4   **Repeat Steps 2 and 3 for the next two artifacts.** Project *Transparency 7D: Things at School: Object 2* and *Transparency 7E: Things at School: Object 3.*

   - After Presenters have shared their groups' ideas, identify Object 2 as a student desk. Explain that, in some schools, two students shared a desk. The seat and the desk were usually fastened to the floor with screws, so they could not be moved around. Ask: *How is this different from schools today?*

   - Identify Object 3 as a lantern. Explain that this type of light was used in the classroom long ago. Some lanterns burned oil, and some burned kerosene. Call attention to the lighting in your own classroom, perhaps by turning the lights off briefly. Ask students to think about whether one little lantern could light up an entire room.

5   **Provide additional information about schools in the past.** Share the following facts. As you share, encourage students to compare each fact about schools in the past with schools today. Ask: *How is this different from today? How is it the same?*

   - Long ago, many people lived on small farms. There would be one small school for all the families in one area. One-room schoolhouses were common because the schools had only a few students at each grade level.

   - A one-room school had only one teacher. Often the teacher didn't have a house but took turns staying with various families in the area. That meant your teacher could be sharing your home.

Transparency 7C

Transparency 7D

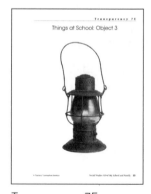

Transparency 7E

- For drinking water, the one-room school had a bucket of water with a tin dipper in it. A dipper was a small cup with a long handle. Everyone drank from the same dipper.

- The bathroom was a small outhouse behind the school. (The same was true for people's homes long ago.)

6 **Read aloud Sections 7.1 and 7.2 in the *Social Studies Alive! My School and Family* Big Book as students follow along.** Introduce the New Ideas *long ago* and *schoolhouse*. Have students respond to the text by looking carefully at the pictures and answering the questions.

7 **Help students organize what they are learning.** Draw a T-chart on the board or on chart paper. Label the columns "Schools Long Ago" and "Schools Now." After the reading, ask students to identify some things that are the same or different about schools long ago and school as they know it today. Write their ideas in the chart.

8 **Have students open their Interactive Student Notebooks to the first page of Reading Notes 7.** Read and model using this two-column chart. Have students work alone or in pairs to complete the chart, drawing two objects from schools in the past and two from schools today.

Phase 2: Examining Artifacts of Student Life in the Past

9 **Continue this Response Group activity with students in the same mixed-ability groups of three.** Assign a new Presenter in each group.

10 **Show another object from the time capsule by projecting *Transparency 7F: Student Life: Object 1.*** As before, do not reveal what the object is.

- Ask groups to talk about what the object is and how it might have been used. When they are ready, have the Presenters share their group's ideas.

- Identify Object 1 as a primer (pronounced *primmer*). Primers were schoolbooks used to teach the alphabet, simple words like *cat* and *fox*, and short sentences. All the pictures in primers were black and white. The primer was usually a child's first (and often only) book. This is how students long ago learned to read.

11 **Repeat Step 9 for *Transparency 7G: Student Life: Object 2* and *Transparency 7H: Student Life: Object 3.***

- After Presenters have shared their groups' ideas, identify Object 2 as a writing slate and a piece of chalk. A slate was made of a thin sheet of dark stone. Writing done with chalk (or, earlier in history, a slate pencil) could be wiped off with a piece of cloth. Explain that students long ago practiced spelling and did number problems on a slate because paper was expensive. Ask: *How is this the same as, and different from, today?*

- Identify Object 3 as a hornbook. A hornbook was a book with just one page. This one sheet of paper was nailed to a piece of wood shaped like a paddle. The alphabet and sometimes a few simple sentences were printed on this page. It was called a *hornbook* because the paper was covered with a very thin, see-through layer of cow's horn, to protect it for repeated use.

Transparency 7F

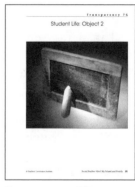

Transparency 7G

Transparency 7H

12 Provide additional information about student life in the past. Share the following facts. As you share, encourage students to compare each fact about children's lives in the past with their lives today. Ask: *How is this different from today? How is it the same?*

- School was in session only a few months each year. That's because long ago, children were needed to work on their family's farm. Winter was the only time they weren't working in the fields, so that's when they went to school.

- Students in a single classroom ranged in age from 4 to 14. Girls sat on one side of the room, and boys sat on the other. When the teacher called on them, they stood up before they answered. They always said, "Yes ma'am" and "No ma'am" or "Yes sir" and "No sir."

- Children did chores at home or on the farm before going to school. They might have fed chickens, collected eggs, milked a cow, or fetched buckets of water from the well.

- Children carried their lunches to school in tin pails. Lunch might have been cold biscuits or cornbread their mother had made, hard-boiled eggs, and fresh or preserved fruit or vegetables that had been grown on their farm.

13 Read aloud Sections 7.3 and 7.4 in the Big Book as students follow along.

- Explain that because old schoolhouses served many children who lived on farms out in the country, farm children sometimes walked as far as one or two miles to school. Unless they were lucky enough to have a horse, there was no other choice—no bikes, no cars, no buses.

- Review the New Idea *hornbook.* Have students look carefully at the pictures and answer the questions. After reading the selections, ask students to identify what is the same and different about daily life and school supplies, long ago and now. Continue to record their answers in the T-chart (from Step 7).

14 Have students turn to the second page of Reading Notes 7 in their Interactive Student Notebooks. Have students work alone or in pairs to complete the page, drawing the objects children used in school long ago and two objects they use in school now.

Reading Further: From Buggies to Blastoff!

1 Introduce the concept of oral histories. Ask: *What if we wanted to learn more about schools long ago, for example, how children got back and forth from home to school? How could we find out? Is there someone we could talk to?* Ask students if they have ever talked to parents or grandparents about what their lives were like when they were young. Discuss the idea that older people are like a "living" time capsule. Some of them have pictures of the past they can share, like the pictures that were in the school time capsule, and they all have stories to tell about their past.

> **Writing Tip: Collaborate on a Writing Project**
> Put students in small groups. Ask each group to choose a classroom object to put in a time capsule about student life today. Each group should identify their object and describe its use. Provide a writing model:
> *This is a* _____.
> *We use it to* _____.
> Assign one group member to illustrate the object, one to write the description, and one to act as the Presenter.

2 **Project *Transparency 7I: Horse and Buggy.*** Ask the following visual discovery questions to help students analyze the image and connect it to what they are about to learn:

Transparency 7I

- What do you see in this picture?

- What do you notice about the road? How do you think it would feel to travel on this road?

- How would you describe this form of transportation? Where do you think the people in the buggy might be going?

- Is this picture from today or from long ago? What makes you think so?

  Tell students that this picture from long ago comes from a story told by a very old man, known to his friends and family as "Mister Bob." Ask: *How old do you think Mister Bob could be?*

3 **Turn to Reading Further 7 in the Big Book and read it aloud while students follow along in their Student Editions.** Ask: *Who is telling this story?* Help students understand that it is told from Mister Bob's point of view.

4 **Ask students about ways transportation has changed over time, as well as ways it has remained the same.** Have them talk about the photographs in "From Buggies to Blastoff!" Encourage students to share any experiences they have had with travel by train, car, or airplane.

5 **Discuss the changes in how people lived that are associated with changes in transportation.**

- Help students recognize that each successive form of transportation that Mister Bob took made travel faster and easier for him. Point out that Mister Bob said when he was little, "We never went much farther than town." Ask: *How did that change for him over the years? How did changes in transportation help Mister Bob see other places in his country, as well as other countries around the world?*

- Discuss with students how communities changed as people began to travel more widely. For example, help them list parts of a community that were not around in horse-and-buggy days (e.g., businesses like gas stations, car repair shops, drive-though restaurants, airports).

- Ask students what changes in transportation they think the future might bring for them.

6 **Review Mister Bob's story in sequence and introduce timelines.** Have students open their Interactive Student Notebooks to Reading Further 7.

- Call attention to Mister Bob's timeline, and read aloud the directions for the first timeline only. Have students trace the timeline across both pages with a finger. Explain that a timeline shows the order in which things happen over time. Point out that this timeline starts when Mister Bob was a little boy (age 5). Explain that each spot along the line shows a later age, continuing all the way up to today (age 99).

- Distribute copies of *Student Handout 7: Cutouts for Mister Bob's Timeline*. Have students cut out the forms of transportation on the handout and match each one to a different age of Mister Bob's life. Allow students to refer to Reading Further 7 in their Student Editions for a reminder of the story sequence.

Student Handout 7

7 **Help students construct a timeline of their own lives.**

- Call attention to the personal timeline below Mister Bob's and read the directions aloud. Point out that there are places on this timeline to draw three things: something from their *past*, something from their *present*, and something from their *future*.

- Have students brainstorm ideas for pictures they could draw of their past. Some students may want to emulate Mister Bob and make their own personal transportation timeline (for example, past: a stroller; present: a bike; future: a car). Some may remember a significant event from kindergarten or preschool.

- For the future picture, students could draw what job they think they will have when they grow up or what they expect to be doing in later years of their school life. As needed, help students choose an appropriate age for their past and future pictures.

8 **For practice in telling a story in sequence, call on volunteers to present the pictures they have drawn.** Encourage them to tell "the story of my life" as they explain, in order, the events or situations they have pictured for past, present, and future.

Processing

1 **Review how schools and student life are the same and different now and in the past.** Encourage students to use the drawings they made in Reading Notes 7 for prompts as they talk about similarities and differences.

- Ask: *What do students need in school? How were those needs met in schools long ago? How are those needs met in schools today?*

- Collect a few suggestions for student needs, such as desks, something to write with, things to read, things to play with at recess. Then ask: *How do you think schools in the future might meet these needs?* Encourage students to be creative in their thinking; their ideas need not be entirely realistic. Record their ideas on the board.

2 **Have students turn to Processing 7 in their Interactive Student Notebooks.** Read the directions aloud. Then have students complete the page, drawing something that future schools might have and writing a sentence to explain how that item would be used.

3 **Have students share their responses with the class.** With Interactive Student Notebooks left open on clean desktops, conduct a gallery walk around the room. Encourage students to comment on their classmates' work, noticing how each idea reflects a change from schools of today.

Vocabulary Development: Place Terms in Sequence

Draw a timeline just above the chalk tray. Mark three points along the line. Make word cards to introduce sets of three words for students to place in order (earliest on the left-hand side). Include sets such as these:
past, present, future
yesterday, today, tomorrow
last year, this year, next year
first, next, last

Assessment

Masters for the chapter assessment appear in the *Lesson Masters*.
Answers appear below.

Big Ideas

1. blue circles: lantern, hornbook, dunce cap
2. red circles: computer, *Space Science* book
3. label 1: horse and buggy

   label 2: old car

   label 3: passenger jet

Show You Know

4. Students should show and label three things in an old-fashioned classroom that are different from their school today.

English Language Learners

Encourage English Language Learners to participate in the Response Group activity. To help them understand the process for the group discussion and what the Presenter does, model the process with the first transparency. Ask the ELL students to serve as Presenters when they are ready to do so. If they are not comfortable summarizing the group's entire discussion, encourage them to say, "Our group agrees" or "Our group disagrees" (with the previous group) and allow a partner to share the remaining information. As the ELL students begin to take ownership and feel invested in the class activity, they will begin to feel more comfortable elaborating on the lesson concepts.

Students with Special Needs

For the Processing activity, help students generate ideas by identifying the categories of school life that were discussed during the lesson: heating, lighting, student seating, tools for reading, tools for writing. Model a comparison of the past, present, and future in terms of these categories, listing them in a three-column chart. For example: *We talked about how schools were heated in the past (a coal-burning stove) and how our school is heated today (oil furnace in the basement). How might a school of the future be heated?*

Enrichment

Use the Reading Further story as a model of the way people who have lived a long time can teach us something about history. As a class, brainstorm interview questions that students could ask older members of their own families, family friends, or neighbors, to obtain information about the past. Help each student write two or three questions on a particular topic, such as cooking and meals, jobs, what children did for fun, houses, telephones, mail, stores and shopping, or any topic of their choice. Then have students conduct their interviews outside of school and write and illustrate a short report on what they learned. If some students have no one to interview, they could work with an adult to find information on their topic in the library or online.

Enrichment Resources

Have students find out more about the past and how to learn things about the past from older people by exploring the following Enrichment Resources for *Social Studies Alive! My School and Family,* at www.learntci.com.

Internet Connections

These recommended Web sites provide useful and engaging content that enforces skills development and mastery of subjects within the chapter.

Enrichment Readings

These in-depth readings encourage students to explore selected topics related to the chapter. For Chapter 7, you may wish to use one or more of the Enrichment Readings listed for the chapter. You may also find readings that relate the chapter's content directly to your state's curriculum.

Additional Reading Opportunities

These fiction and nonfiction books, which can be read aloud to students, offer opportunities to extend the content in this chapter.

Going to School by Philip Steele (Danbury, CT: Franklin Watts, 2002)

The history of schools—from ancient times to the classroom of today—is presented in this reference that teachers can share with students. Information on school uniforms, the hornbook, dame schools, one-room schoolhouses, and playgrounds is supported with illustrations and photographs.

If You Lived 100 Years Ago by Ann McGovern. Illustrated by Anna DiVito. (New York: Scholastic, 1999)

This compelling look at New York City as it was 100 years ago helps the young reader see where people lived and worked, what they wore, what they ate, how they traveled, and many other aspects of everyday city life in the past.

McGuffey's Eclectic Primer, Revised Edition. (New York: Jossey-Bass, 1997)

This reproduction of a widely used beginning reader, first copyrighted in 1881, offers today's first graders a real taste of the past. Students can compare the vocabulary, stories, and illustrations with those found in the reading books in their own classroom.

When I Was Little: A Four-Year-Old's Memoir of Her Youth by Jamie Lee Curtis. Illustrated by Laura Cornell. (New York: HarperTrophy, 1995)

This account of being a baby, told through the eyes of a preschooler, will help students remember things about their own past in order to create a simple timeline of their life.

On the left, draw two objects you would find in a school long ago. On the right, draw two objects you would find in a school now.

Schools Long Ago	Schools Now
1 Answers will vary. Possible drawings for the two boxes in this column include a coal stove, an oil lantern, and a bucket and dipper.	**1** Answers will vary. Possible drawings for the two boxes in this column include whiteboard and markers, electric lights, and drinking fountains.
2	**2**

On the left, draw two objects children used
in school long ago. On the right, draw two
objects children use in school now.

Student Life Long Ago	Student Life Now
1 Answers will vary. Possible drawings for the two boxes in this column include hornbooks, slates, and primers.	**1** Answers will vary. Possible drawings for the two boxes in this column include picture books, colored markers, and lined paper.
2	**2**

What Groups Do We Belong To?

Overview

Students learn about groups to which they may belong: school, family, and community. In the Preview, students think of two activities they do with other people. In a Social Studies Skill Builder, they identify and categorize different types of groups. In Reading Further, they consider the many groups an American Indian girl belongs to and the special things she has learned from them. In a Processing activity, students draw and write about three groups to which they belong.

Objectives

Social Studies

- Identify family, school, and community groups.
- Sort pictures according to specified criteria.
- Apply knowledge about groups to one's own life.

Language Arts

- Explain reasons for a choice. (speaking)
- Identify main ideas and details in the text. (reading)

Social Studies Vocabulary

school, family, community

Materials

Social Studies Alive! My School and Family Big Book and Student Editions

Transparencies 8A–8B

Placards 8A–8L

Interactive Student Notebooks

Lesson Masters

- Student Handouts 8A–8C
- Information Master 8

CD Track 8
envelopes

Time Estimates

Preview: 30 min.

Social Studies Skill Builder: 2 sessions (30 min. each)

Reading Further: 30 min.

Processing: 30 min.

Activity	Suggested Time	Materials
Preview • Connecting to Prior Knowledge • Building Background Knowledge • Developing Vocabulary	30 minutes	• Interactive Student Notebooks
Social Studies Skill Builder Identifying and categorizing types of groups	30-minute sessions (2) • Sorting groups by type (Steps 1–5) • Learning more about three types of groups (Steps 6 and 7)	• *Social Studies Alive! My School and Family* Big Book and Student Editions, Sections 8.1–8.4 • Transparency 8A • Placards 8A–8L • Interactive Student Notebooks • Student Handouts 8A–8C (1 of each, cut apart, per pair) • envelopes (1 per pair)
Reading Further Exploring one girl's groups and the things she has learned from them	30 minutes	• *Social Studies Alive! My School and Family* Big Book, Chapter 8 Reading Further • Transparency 8B • Interactive Student Notebooks
Processing Drawing and writing about one's own groups	30 minutes	• Interactive Student Notebooks • Information Master 8 (1 per pair, optional) • CD Track 8
Assessment	15 minutes	• Chapter 8 Assessment, Lesson Masters • Chapter 8 Assessment, Digital Teacher Resources

Preview

1 **Connecting to Prior Knowledge:** Help students recall their prior experience with being in groups.

- Have students open their Interactive Student Notebooks to Preview 8. Tell them to list two activities that they do with other people. For each activity, ask them to draw a picture to show a number of people taking part in the activity with them.

- Ask volunteers to share their activities. Make a list on the board of the different group activities that students identify.

2 **Building Background Knowledge:** Introduce the concept of belonging to a group.

- Select three students who are wearing clothing of the same color and have them stand at the front of the room. Tell the class that these three students have something in common, and have students guess what it is. Explain that because the three students have something in common, they form a group. Tell students that a group has more than one person in it and that the people in a group have something in common. Refer to the activities you listed on the board in Step 1 and point out that they are all done by groups of people.

- Play *Do You Belong in This Group?* to reinforce students' understanding of what a group is. Choose four students who have something in common (all wearing sneakers, for example) and have them stand at the front of the room. Then ask students to raise their hands silently if they think they belong in this group, without saying aloud why they think so. If any student wearing sneakers raises a hand, say that he or she does belong in the group and may join it. If a student wearing another type of shoe raises a hand, say that he or she does not belong in this group. After several students have joined the group, ask what the group has in common. Remind students of the characteristics of a group.

3 **Developing Vocabulary:** Cover New Ideas—*school, family,* and *community*—as they arise in the text. You may want to discuss some terms before beginning the activity, using methods described in *Solutions for Effective Instruction.*

> **Reading Strategy:**
> **Use an Anticipation Guide**
>
> Provide this list of true-or-false statements for use as an anticipation guide.
>
> 1. A group has more than one person. (T or F)
>
> 2. There are big and small groups at school. (T or F)
>
> 3. A family can be two people. (T or F)
>
> 4. A baseball team is not a group. (T or F)

Social Studies Skill Builder

1 **Prepare for the activity.** For each pair of students, copy *Student Handouts 8A–8C: Four Family Groups, Four School Groups,* and *Four Community Groups,* cut apart the four pictures on each, and place all twelve pictures in an envelope, in mixed order.

2 **Introduce three groups to which all students belong.** Turn through Sections 8.1–8.4 of the *Social Studies Alive! My School and Family* Big Book. Read aloud each page's heading only and focus attention on the photographs and drawings.

Student Handouts 8A–8C

- Ask students to describe the group shown in each photograph, telling what the people have in common and how many people are in the group.

- Then ask: *What three types of groups did these pages show?* As students name the groups, write the words *school, family,* and *community* on the board and have students read them aloud with you.

- Project *Transparency 8A: What Groups Do We Belong To?* Ask students to point to each group shown in the picture and tell what kind of group it is (one school group, two family groups, and one community group—the baseball team).

Transparency 8A

3 **Have students sort pictures to categorize groups as *school, family,* or *community.*** Assign students to mixed-ability pairs and give each pair an envelope of pictures.

- Call attention to the three words on the board (*school, family, and community*) and tell students that their envelope includes pictures of all three groups. Explain that you want them to sort their pictures into three piles: a school pile, a family pile, and a community pile. Pairs should look carefully at each picture and decide together which type of group it shows.

- When students have finished categorizing the pictures, check that they have done so correctly. If a pair has miscategorized any pictures, ask why they placed them where they did. Students may have different interpretations of some photographs, so be sure to acknowledge good reasoning about the categories.

- Challenge students to sort the pictures in other ways—for example, by number of people shown (line up pictures from the most to the fewest in the group) or by background (indoor and outdoor scenes).

4 **Have students match placards to words to identify groups.**

- Distribute one of *Placards 8A–8L: Groups 1–12* to each pair.

- Ask pairs to look carefully at their placard, decide which group (family, school, or community) it shows, and then discuss how they know. As a check for understanding, ask pairs to bring their placard to the front of the class and tell which category it belongs in and why. Students can categorize the placards by placing each one under the correct word on the board.

Placards 8A–8L

5 **Help students consider as a whole all the groups they categorized.** With all 12 placards spread along the chalk rail, ask students to stand in a line in front of the placard that shows their favorite picture. Ask several students to share which group they chose and what that group means to them. (**Note:** You might want to have CD Track 8, "We Belong to Groups," playing in the background during this part of the activity.)

6 **Help students read about and recognize the different type of groups to which they belong.**

- Read Section 8.1 aloud while students follow along in their Student Editions. Then ask students to stand if they belong to a group (all should stand). Ask several volunteers to name one of their groups.

- To review school groups, read Section 8.2 aloud as students follow along. Ask students to stand if they belong to a school group (all should stand). Then ask them to sit if they belong to a class group (all should sit). Have students name some other types of school groups, such as reading groups, table groups, and after-school groups.

- To review family groups, read Section 8.3 aloud as students follow along. Then ask students to stand if they belong to a family group (all should stand). Then ask volunteers to report how many people are in their family group or who the members are.

- To review community groups, read Section 8.4 aloud as students follow along. Then ask students to name community groups that they belong to or would like to join. As needed, suggest some examples: sports teams, religious groups, singing groups, or youth organizations such as 4-H.

7 **Have students identify and write about the three types of groups.** Read the Summary aloud as students follow along. Then have students turn to Reading Notes 8 in their Interactive Student Notebooks. Read the directions together. Have students complete the page, identifying the three groups pictured.

Transparency 8B

Reading Further: My Groups

1 **Project** *Transparency 8B: A Special Group.* Cover the images on the right and direct attention to the image at the left. Ask:

- What do you see in this picture?

- What do you see growing?

- What group of people do you think you might find in a place like this?

Then uncover the two images on the right and ask:

- What do you see in these pictures? What do you think the woman in the canoe is doing?

- How do you think these pictures are connected to the one on the left?

2 **Tell students that the group connected to both pictures is American Indian basket weavers.** These particular baskets were made by women in California. Explain that the left picture shows a special kind of plant that grows in California, called tule (pronounced TOO-lee). Tule looks like a very tall grass. It grows in wet places, such as marshland and along the edge of lakes. Women like the one in the canoe pick tule and other plants they find in nature. Then they weave these into beautiful baskets. Provide this additional information:

- When the women weavers gather what they need to make baskets, they show respect for Earth. For example, they are careful not to take more than they need or to gather too much tule from one single place or too many branches from one tree. They want to leave the land as healthy as they found it. This is the way of their people.

Reading Strategy: Identify Main Idea

After reading each section, have students identify one sentence on the page that best states the main idea of the page. They should discover that in each case, the section title is the best statement of the main idea. Then ask them to find two details on each page that support the main idea.

- American Indians were the first people to live in North America, thousands of years ago. They lived very close to nature and they knew how important nature was to their survival. They met all their needs for food, clothing, and shelter by carefully using the woods and fields and the animals, birds, and fish who lived there. American Indians were thankful for all growing, living things. They believed in the importance of respecting and protecting the Earth.

- For American Indians, the family and the tribe are both very important groups. Long ago, American Indian children did not go to school the way you do today. Families and older people in their tribe taught the children everything they needed to know—about finding food, making their own clothing and homes, and using tools. The things that you learn from your groups are all part of the kind of person you become.

3 **Open the Big Book to *Reading Further 8: My Groups*.** Tell students that this story is told by a girl who, like them, belongs to many groups. Read the story aloud as students follow along in their Student Editions. After reading, ask:

- What are some of Naomi's groups?

- Which of her groups are like the groups that you are part of?

- Which of her groups are different from your groups?

- What are some things that Naomi has learned from her groups?

- Naomi has learned something from her family group that she will pass on to her own children if she has a daughter some day. What is it?

- What is important about Naomi's middle name? Do any of you have a name that came from another member of your family? What about your last name?

(**Note:** See the Internet Connections for this chapter if you would like to share further information about the basket weavers in Naomi's family, who lived in Yosemite National Park for many years. They continue to demonstrate their skills and share with park visitors their philosophy of staying connected to the past and to the environment.)

4 **Help students understand the ways in which American Indian groups pass on their knowledge from one generation to the next.** Give some examples of native legends, perhaps focusing on tribes in your local area. Explain that long ago, stories like these were not written down, but were shared as spoken tales, told by storytellers while an audience listened. (**Note:** The Additional Reading Opportunities for this chapter include some legends that are suitable as read-alouds for further discussion.)

5 **Ask students to consider the kinds of knowledge or traditions that are being passed down within their own family group.** Have students turn to Reading Further 8 in their Interactive Student Notebooks.

- Read aloud the directions. Then help students brainstorm ideas for things they have learned, things they might teach their own children some day. These might include types of cooking, crafts, games, music, or stories. They can use these ideas to complete the sentence and drawing.

Processing

1   **Review the three group categories by playing CD Track 8, "We Belong to Groups."** Teach students the words of the song, referring to the lyrics on *Information Master 8: We Belong to Groups.*

2   **Introduce the Processing activity.** Have students open their Interactive Student Notebooks to Processing 8. Read the directions aloud, pointing out that there are three pages to this activity. Model by drawing on the board a simple picture of one school group you belong to, such as a group of teachers. As you draw, ask students to help you decide what details (for example, background, clothing, or objects) to add to your drawing.

3   **Have students illustrate and write about three groups to which they belong.** They should complete Processing 8 independently.

-   Encourage students to include a background and a few details about each group in their drawings. Suggest that they mention some of these details in their sentences.

-   If some students do not belong to a community group such as Cub Scouts or a sports team, suggest that they draw a picture of a community group they would like to join. Also remind them that all the people of their city or town are one large community group.

Assessment

Masters for the chapter assessment appear in the *Lesson Masters.* Answers appear below.

Big Ideas

1. school group: picture of teacher and classroom

    family group: picture of family picnic

    community group: picture of t-ball game

2. circle: the basket

Show You Know

3. The bulleted points can serve as a two-point rubric.

Information Master 8

Speaking and Listening: Personalize Song Lyrics

Hand out copies of Information Master 8 and have pairs work together to think of a new last line for each verse, describing a group to which they belong; for example, for the school verse: "We both go to Franklin School." Replay Track 8, asking volunteers to sing or chant their new line on cue.

English Language Learners

During the Building Background Knowledge activity, include English language learners in the groups you choose in the game *Do You Belong in This Group?* As students discuss what people in a group have in common, allow English language learners to point to rather than name the shared characteristic (e.g., shoe type, shirt color). Then provide the appropriate words to identify the common characteristic and have students repeat them with you. Then have them point to the same item on another student and say whether that student belongs in the group, repeating the identifying words each time.

Students with Special Needs

After students draw their three pictures in the Processing activity, allow them to dictate their sentences if they have difficulty writing the words themselves. Then help students read the words aloud, check for sense, and work with them to revise the sentences if needed.

Enrichment

Have students interview five people outside the classroom (parents, siblings, neighbors, friends) and ask each person to name three groups to which he or she belongs. After students collect the data, have them classify each response as a family, school, or community group. Hold a discussion of their findings, helping them identify patterns, similarities, and differences. Encourage the students to draw conclusions such as these: *People still belong to groups as adults. Children and adults can belong to the same groups. More adults belong to community groups than the kids in our class do.*

Enrichment Resources

Have students find out more about groups by exploring the following Enrichment Resources for *Social Studies Alive! My School and Family,* at www.learntci.com.

Internet Connections

These recommended Web sites provide useful and engaging content that enforces skills development and mastery of subjects within the chapter.

Enrichment Readings

These in-depth readings encourage students to explore selected topics related to the chapter. For Chapter 8, you may wish to use one or more of the Enrichment Readings listed for the chapter. You may also find readings that relate the chapter's content directly to your state's curriculum.

Additional Reading Opportunities

The following fiction and nonfiction books, which can be read aloud to students, offer opportunities to extend the content in this chapter.

Celebrating Families by Rosmarie Hausherr (New York: Scholastic Press, 1997)
Fourteen photo-essays of real children foster an appreciation of the diversity found in family groups, including a mother with a disability, a family in a shelter, and children in foster care.

Franklin Plays the Game by Paulette Bourgeois. Illustrated by Brenda Clark. (Toronto: Kids Can Press, 1995)

A young turtle and his teammates, who have been losing every soccer game, learn how to practice and work together. This story celebrates the value of teamwork and the fun of playing on a team, win or lose.

Stagestruck by Tomie dePaola (New York: Puffin Books, 2007)

Tommy ruffles some feathers when he upstages his fellow actors in the class play. This humorous story underscores the importance of being a good member of a group.

American Indian Legends

Coyote: A Trickster Tale from the American Southwest by Gerald McDermott (New York: Voyager Books, 1999)

The trickster character is common in American Indian folklore. In this adaptation of a Zuni tale, Coyote decides he wants to learn how to fly but falls victim to the crows who first humor him, then outwit him.

How Chipmunk Got His Stripes by Joseph Bruchac and James Bruchac. Illustrated by Jose Aruego and Ariane Dewey. (New York: Puffin Books, 2003)

This is an example of the pourquoi tale, which offers an explanation for an element in nature. This particular tale has Iroquois, Cherokee, Abenaki and Mohawk versions. The father-son storytelling team are committed to the preservation of native legends.

How the Stars Fell into the Sky: A Navajo Legend by Jerrie Oughton. Illustrated by Lisa Desimini. (Boston: Hougton Mifflin, 1996)

The retelling of a pourquoi tale from the Navajo explains the disorder of the stars scattered through the night sky.

The Legend of the Indian Paintbrush retold by Tomie dePaola (New York: Putnam Juvenile, 1996)

This pourquoi tale from the Plains Indians explains how a beautiful wildflower came to be.

Legends of the Seminoles as told by Betty Mae Jumper. Illustrated by Guy LaBree. (Sarasota: Pineapple Press, 1994)

Stories and legends retold by a Seminole elder impart lessons about living in harmony with Florida's natural environment.

Turtle's Race with Beaver as told by Joseph Bruchac and James Bruchac. Illustrated by Jose Aruego and Ariane Dewey. (New York: Puffin Books, 2005)

Students may recognize the similarities with Aesop's *The Tortoise and The Hare* in this classic tale of brains versus brawn, adapted from the Seneca oral tradition.

Choose a word. Write it next to its picture.

Then write a sentence about that group.

School	Family	Community

Community

Students' sentences will vary but should describe

this community group.

School

Students' sentences will vary but should describe

this school group.

Family

Students' sentences will vary but should describe

this family group.

How Are Families Special?

Overview

Students learn that all families are special in different ways. In the Preview activity, they consider what their families mean to them. In a Writing for Understanding activity, students read about different family members, types of homes, and family activities. They then create a book to share how their own families are special. In Reading Further, they learn that communities across the country are also special in different ways. The writing activity serves as the Processing assignment for the chapter.

Objectives

Social Studies

- Use relationship terms (e.g. *mother, brother, cousin*) to identify family roles.
- Name examples for three categories of family attributes (family roles, types of home, and types of activity).
- Compare and contrast communities in terms of their physical features, climate, and human activities.

Language Arts

- Write a booklet about one's own family. (writing)

Social Studies Vocabulary

family members, homes, activities

Materials

Social Studies Alive! My School and Family Big Book and Student Editions

Transparencies 9A and 9B

Interactive Student Notebooks

Lesson Masters

- Student Handouts 9A–9D

Time Estimates

Preview: 20 min.

Writing for Understanding: 6 sessions (30 min. each)

Reading Further: 25 min.

Activity	Suggested Time	Materials
Preview • Connecting to Prior Knowledge • Developing Vocabulary • Building Background Knowledge	20 minutes	• Interactive Student Notebooks
Writing for Understanding Comparing families—who their members are, where they live, and what they do together	30-minute sessions (6) • Reading: Family members (Steps 1–4) • Writing: Family members (Step 5) • Reading: Homes (Steps 6 and 7) • Writing: Homes (Step 8) • Reading: Activities (Steps 9 and 10) • Writing: Activities (Steps 11 and 12)	• *Social Studies Alive! My School and Family* Big Book and Student Editions, Chapter 9 introduction and Sections 9.1–9.4 • Transparency 9A • Interactive Student Notebooks • Student Handouts 9A–9D (1 of each per student)
Reading Further Comparing communities and identifying the features that make them special	25 minutes	• *Social Studies Alive! My School and Family* Big Book and Student Editions, Chapter 9 Reading Further • Transparency 9B • Interactive Student Notebooks
Processing Creating the Family Book serves as the Processing activity for this chapter.		
Assessment	15 minutes	• Chapter 9 Assessment, Lesson Masters • Chapter 9 Assessment, Digital Teacher Resources

Preview

1. **Connecting to Prior Knowledge:** Remind students of the three groups—school, family, and community—they learned about in the previous chapter. Tell them that they are now going to look more closely at one of those groups, families.

   - Have students open their Interactive Student Notebooks to Preview 9. Read the directions aloud.

   - Help students brainstorm words they might add to the web to show what *family* means to them. Start a word bank on the board. You might ask: *What are some things you do with your family? What are some things you say to each other? How do you feel about the people in your family?*

   - Give students a few minutes to complete their webs. Then ask if any of them want to share their ideas about what a family is. Help them agree on this general definition: "A family is a group of people who love and care for one another."

2. **Developing Vocabulary:** Cover New Ideas—*family members, homes,* and *activities*—as they arise in the text. You may want to discuss some terms before beginning the activity, using methods described in *Solutions for Effective Instruction.*

3. **Building Background Knowledge:** Start a discussion about the ways in which families are different.

   - Use the introduction to Chapter 9 in the *Social Studies Alive! My School and Family* Big Book or project *Transparency 9A: How Are Families Special?* Ask students to point out the different families pictured. Explain that these families are alike in that they all love and care for one another. Ask students to guess how these families might be different from one another. Write their ideas on the board, grouping them into three categories—family members, homes, and activities—if appropriate.

   - Turn through Chapter 9 in the Big Book, reading aloud just the section headings. Pause on each page to have students look carefully at the pictures and talk about what they see. After this preview of the chapter, suggest an expanded definition of family: "A family is a group of people who love and care for one another. Families are all special in different ways."

Writing for Understanding

1. **Prepare writing materials before class.** Staple together *Student Handouts 9A–9D: Family Book* to make one book for each student. Create a model that tells about your own family.

2. **Tell students that they will now learn some terms we use to name the members of a family.** Read Sections 9.1 and 9.2 in the Big Book as students follow along in their Student Editions.

Vocabulary Development: Use a Word Wall

Begin a family word wall. Add new vocabulary words associated with families as they are introduced. Students may refer to the word wall during oral activities and when they are writing. This will encourage them to use the new terms. Continue to build this word wall through the next five chapters.

Transparency 9A

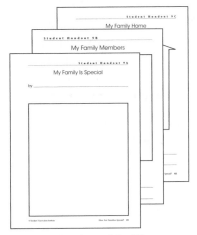

Student Handouts 9A–9D

- After reading Section 9.1, review the idea that all families are special in different ways. Ask students to describe the family pictured: *Is this family big or small? What do you think they like to do together?*

- After reading Section 9.2, ask students to apply family terms (such as *mother, father, son, daughter, sister, brother*) to the people pictured in Sections 9.1 and 9.2. Then ask them to name the members of their own families. If a student refers to a family member by a proper name, help the student identify his or her relationship to that person. List family terms on the board.

3 **Project Transparency 9A again.** Ask students to name the members of each family in the picture. If any new family terms are mentioned, add them to the list on the board.

- Use the pictured families to start a discussion of the roles that different members of a family may play and the way these roles may vary from one family to another. For example, ask: *Which family members work to earn money to buy things for the family? Which family members shop for food? Which family members take care of things around the house? Which family members take care of the youngest children?*

- If one student assigns a particular role to a particular family member, ask if anyone else has a family in which people have different roles. Help students understand that in every family, people participate in different ways to take care of things for the family.

4 **Have students write terms identifying four different family relationships.** Ask them to complete Reading Notes 9, Part A, in their Interactive Student Notebooks, identifying any four family members. Have students work in pairs. Remind them to refer to the family word wall or to the lists on the board.

5 **Introduce the Family Book, in which students will draw and identify the members of their own families.** Share the model you created. Then distribute a prepared blank book to each student.

- Have students turn to the "My Family Members" page. Explain that they will work on the cover after they have finished writing their books.

- Tell students to draw a picture that shows each member of their family. For simplicity, you might suggest that they draw only the family members who live with them, but allow students to interpret this any way that makes them comfortable. Then have them complete the sentence, "The members of my family are...."

6 **Introduce the idea that families live in different types of homes.** Read Section 9.3 as students follow along. Ask students to tell what they know about the different types of homes mentioned in this section.

- Help students identify both apartment buildings and single-family homes in the photograph on this page. Explain that these homes are in a city, so they are very close together. Homes in smaller towns are often spread farther apart, with yards around them. Homes in the country usually sit by themselves, with no neighboring homes for miles around.

> **Reading Strategy: Make Inferences**
>
> Point out that to name the members of each family pictured, students must make inferences. That means they must use clues from the picture, plus what they know about families, to make a good guess. Ask students to support their inferences by describing the clues they used.

- Project Transparency 9A again as an example of homes with yards. Ask students about any differences they see in the homes pictured here (e.g., one-story/two-story, wood/brick, porch/no porch).

- Ask for volunteers to share the type of home they live in. Write their responses on the board. Encourage them to talk about ways their homes differ from the homes pictured in their Student Editions.

7 **Have students identify three different types of homes.** Ask them to turn to Reading Notes 9, Part B. Have students work in pairs to complete only Part B, identifying three kinds of homes.

8 **Have students create the "My Family Home" page in their Family Book.** Explain that their picture may show either their entire home or their favorite place in their home. Then have them finish the sentence, "My favorite place at home is...." If some students have two homes, encourage them to draw two places if they don't wish to choose.

9 **Introduce the idea that different families enjoy different kinds of activities.** Read aloud Section 9.4 as students follow along.

- Ask students to identify the activities they see on this page. Start a list of family activities on the board. Discuss the fact that sometimes what families like to do for fun will depend on where they live. That is, some families may go to dig clams at the beach, but that's not a choice if you don't live near the ocean. Some families like to go to wild animal parks, but that isn't a choice for everyone; it depends on where you live.

- Project Transparency 9A again for a discussion of the family activities shown. Ask students to point out things that these families are doing together for fun, as well as things they are doing as chores. Then ask students to name things that they like to do with their families, either for fun or to help out at home. Continue adding activities to the list on the board.

10 **Have students name three types of family activities.** Ask them to turn to Reading Notes 9, Part C. Read aloud the directions. Have students work in pairs to complete the page, identifying three family activities.

11 **Have students create the "My Family Activities" page in their Family Book.**

- Explain that the picture should show their family doing a favorite activity together. Remind them to complete the sentence to tell about it.

- When students complete their last page, have them work on the cover. Show them where they should write their names, reminding them to use their best printing. Discuss how students might decorate their book covers.

12 **To encourage the appreciation of family differences, set up a "sharing spot" in the classroom.** This can be any place where students can sit comfortably and read their books to one another. Divide the class into pairs. Announce that when both partners have completed their books and had them checked by the teacher, they may go to the "sharing spot" and read quietly to each other.

Reading Further: Postcard Pen Pals

1 Project *Transparency 9B: Postcard Pen Pals.* Cover the bottom image. Ask the following visual discovery questions about the top image:

   • What do you see in this picture?

   • What kind of buildings do you see?

   • What does that tell you about the kind of place this is?

   Then uncover the bottom image and ask:

   • What do you see in this picture?

   • What kind of buildings do you see?

   • What does that tell you about the kind of place this is?

   Tell students that the story they are about to read will tell them a little about where these very different places are and about the children whose families live there.

2 **Introduce six distinctly different communities where families live.** Read aloud Reading Further 9 in the Big Book while students follow along. After reading each page, ask students to find details in the photograph that support something you read about in the text. Help them identify both natural physical features of the environment (mountains, lakes, rock formations) and human features (buildings, homes, streets).

3 **Help students compare and contrast the places represented by the postcards.** Start four lists on the board, labeled *Land and Water, Weather, Jobs,* and *Food.*

   • Help students look through the text to find examples to list under each category. They will notice that not every child's postcard mentions all of the categories.

   • After listing students' responses under the appropriate label, discuss the ways in which some listed items are linked to a particular place. For example, do they think Grace's dad would have the same job (logger) if he lived in New York City or in the Utah desert?

   • Then ask: *Can you find one thing that is the same about all these children's lives?* (They all go to school.) *What is different about the ways they get to school?* (walking, biking, taking the school bus, and being homeschooled, as well as the weather issues they confront)

   • Ask students if they have visited any of these locations, or places somewhat like them, on a family trip or vacation.

4 **Ask students to compare the places shown on the postcards with their own community.** Ask: *Which one of these places is most like where we live? How is it the same? In what ways is our community different from all these places?* Organize students' ideas on the board, in two lists: "How these places are the same as [name of your community]" and "How these places are different from [your community]."

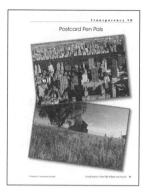

Transparency 9B

> **Reading Strategy: Read Compound Words**
>
> Write on the board these compound words from the text: *postcard, sunflower, rowboat, outside, inside, roadside.* Divide each word into two parts. Point to the shorter words in each compound and ask students to read them aloud separately, then as a compound word.

5   **Help students identify special features of your community.** Have them turn
to Reading Further 9 in their Interactive Student Notebooks. Read the directions aloud. Refer students to the ideas they generated in class about how
their community differs from the ones they saw on the postcards. As needed,
brainstorm further ideas about distinctive local landforms, weather, buildings, parks, and other special places in your community to help them create
their own postcards.

Assessment

Masters for the chapter assessment appear in the *Lesson Masters*.
Answers appear below.

Big Ideas

1. blue circle: family having picnic

2. red circle: house

3. Kansas farm postcard: I live on a farm.

   New York City postcard: I live in a city.

   Utah desert postcard: I live in a desert.

Show You Know

4. "Show your family" and "[show them] doing something for fun" can serve as
   a two-point rubric.

English Language Learners

As students complete the drawing for each page in their Family Books, have them dictate their responses to complete the sentence for each page. Write the caption for them on the first line. Then have students copy the sentence on the line below, for practice reading and writing the words.

Students with Special Needs

Provide support for the writing portions of the lesson—the Family Book and the postcard in the Reading Further activity. Have students draw the pictures and dictate the text they want into a tape recorder. After a teacher, assistant, or parent volunteer transcribes the text onto paper, students can read their words while listening to the tape, thereby reviewing the concepts with both visual and auditory input.

Enrichment

Write the words *spring, summer, fall,* and *winter* on the board. Have students draw from two to four pictures that they could send to a pen pal to show the activities they do with their families and how they dress as the seasons change in their particular community. They can use Extra Student Work pages in the Interactive Student Notebooks for their pictures. Students should title each picture "[Community name] in [name of season]" and write one or more sentences describing what is special about that season where they live. Have volunteers share their work to start a class discussion of the local climate.

Enrichment Resources

Have students find out more about the variation and similarities among families and communities by exploring the following Enrichment Resources for *Social Studies Alive! My School and Family,* at www.learntci.com.

Internet Connections

These recommended Web sites provide useful and engaging content that enforces skills development and mastery of subjects within the chapter.

Enrichment Readings

These in-depth readings encourage students to explore selected topics related to the chapter. For Chapter 9, you may wish to use one or more of the Enrichment Readings listed for the chapter. You may also find readings that relate the chapter's content directly to your state's curriculum.

Additional Reading Opportunities

The following fiction and nonfiction books, which can be read aloud to students, offer opportunities to extend the content in this chapter.

Family by Isabell Monk. Illustrated by Janice Lee Porter. (Minneapolis: Carolrhoda Books, 2005)

Through this story of a family reunion picnic, students learn how families gather for social occasions and also discover that treasured family recipes can be part of what makes a family special.

Listen to the City by Rachel Isadora (New York: G. P. Putnam's Sons, 2000)

This book explores the many different noises that characterize a busy city. Read this with *Night in the Country* (below) to start a discussion of the contrast between living in urban and rural communities.

My Family: Love and Care, Give and Share by Lisa Bullard. Illustrated by Brandon Reibeling. (Minneapolis: Picture Window Books, 2003)

While drawing a picture of his family for school, Matthew finds that after a remarriage, his family is much larger than it once was. This book helps students understand family as "the people you belong with."

Night in the Country by Cynthia Rylant. Illustrated by Mary Szilagyi. (New York: Aladdin, 1991)

Through evocative text and drawings, this book captures much of what is special about life in the countryside. Pair this title with *Listen to the City,* above.

Part A. Family Members

Name four different family members.

Answers may vary. Possible answers: mom, dad, brother, sister, cousin

Part B. Family Homes

Name three kinds of homes.

Answers may vary. Possible answers: apartments, houses, mobile homes

_____

_____

Part C. Family Activities

Name three family activities.

Answers may vary. Possible answers: picnic, movies, fishing

What Do Families Need and Want?

Overview

Students learn what families need and want. In the Preview activity, they think of typical family purchases. The teacher lists these in categories for students to identify, and then helps students distinguish between needs and wants. In a Problem Solving Groupwork activity, students create camping triaramas (three-dimensional scenes) that depict what families would need and want on a camping trip. In Reading Further, students learn about jobs people do to earn money to meet their needs and wants. In the Processing activity, students explain why selected items are needs and wants.

Objectives

Social Studies

- Distinguish between needs as things we must have to live and wants as things it would be nice to have.
- Identify food, clothing, and shelter as needs each family has.
- Describe jobs that people do to earn money to meet their needs and wants.
- Identify items a family might need and want while away from home.

Language Arts

- Make an oral presentation of a group project. (speaking)
- Retell events in sequence. (listening and speaking)
- Support a choice. (writing)

Social Studies Vocabulary

need, want

Materials

Social Studies Alive! My School and Family Big Book and Student Editions

Transparencies 10A–10H

Interactive Student Notebooks

Lesson Masters

- Information Masters 10A–10D
- Student Handout 10

CD Track 9

game markers

construction paper

Time Estimates

Preview: 30 min.

Problem Solving Groupwork: 5 sessions (varying lengths)

Reading Further: 25 min.

Processing: 30 min.

Activity	Suggested Time	Materials
Preview • Connecting to Prior Knowledge • Building Background Knowledge • Developing Vocabulary	30 minutes	• Interactive Student Notebooks • *Social Studies Alive! My School and Family* Big Book, Chapter 10 introduction and Sections 10.1–10.4 • Information Master 10A (1 transparency) • CD Track 9
Problem Solving Groupwork Identifying and categorizing families' needs and wants	*Phase 1* 30-minute sessions (2) • Learning about needs and wants (Steps 1 and 2) • Identifying needs and wants (Steps 3–5) *Phase 2* 30-minute session • Planning a triarama (Steps 6–11) 40-minute session • Creating the triarama (Step 12) 20-minute session • Presenting the work (Step 13)	• *Social Studies Alive! My School and Family* Student Editions, Sections 10.1–10.4 • Transparency 10A • Interactive Student Notebooks • Information Master 10B (1 copy, cut apart) • game markers (several per student) • Transparencies 10B–10G • Placards 10A–10C (3 sets) • Information Master 10C and 10D (1 transparency of each) • Student Handout 10 (1 copy per group of 3 students) • construction paper (one sheet, 12 inches square, per group of 3, plus scraps)
Reading Further Discovering some jobs that people do to earn money in order to meet their families' needs and wants	25 minutes	• *Social Studies Alive! My School and Family* Big Book and Student Editions, Chapter 10 Reading Further • Transparency 10H • Interactive Student Notebooks
Processing Justifying particular items as needs or wants	30 minutes	• Interactive Student Notebooks • CD Track 9
Assessment	15 minutes	• Chapter 10 Assessment, Lesson Masters • Chapter 10 Assessment, Digital Teacher Resources

Preview

1 **Connecting to Prior Knowledge:** Prepare students to understand that the things families buy can be categorized as *food, clothing, shelter,* or *other*.

- Have students open their Interactive Student Notebooks to Preview 10. Read the directions aloud and ask volunteers to name a couple of things that families might buy with their money. To encourage a variety of responses, suggest local stores where families might typically spend money (e.g., bakery, furniture store, department store). Then have students complete the page, drawing and writing four things people buy.

- While students are working in their notebooks, draw a chart with four columns on the board. Number the columns to stand for these hidden categories: 1, "Food"; 2, "Clothing"; 3, "Shelter"; 4, "Other Things."

- Ask students to give examples of things families buy. Write their responses in the appropriate categories on the chart (e.g., *shoes* in Column 2; *books* in Column 4). As you write their ideas in the chart, place nonessential items, such as ice cream or toys, in the "Other Things" column, which will later be categorized as wants.

- Have students guess the column heads. Read the items in the first column, and then ask: *What should we call this column?* Repeat for each column. Students may need your help to come up with the title "Other Things." If any column has very few listings, brainstorm a few more with students once they know the category.

2 **Building Background Knowledge:** Introduce the distinction between needs and wants.

- Open to Chapter 10 in the *Social Studies Alive! My School and Family* Big Book and read the chapter title. Then turn through the pages of Sections 10.1 through 10.4, reading just the section title on each page. Have students discuss the photographs and how they relate to the section titles.

- Tell students that some of the items they listed in the chart (Step 1) are things families *need* to live. Others are things that families don't need but that would be nice to have—things that they *want*. Point to Column 1. Ask students to give you a "thumbs up" if families need these things to live and a "thumbs down" if they don't. Repeat this for each column.

- Explain that the first three columns list needs because families need food, clothing, and shelter to live. Write "Needs" over the first three columns. Explain that the last column lists things that families want but don't need. Write "Wants" over the last column.

- Play CD Track 9, "Needs and Wants." Project a transparency of the song lyrics on *Information Master 10A: Needs and Wants,* and help students follow the words as they listen to the song. Repeat until students are familiar with the words, and then have them sing along.

Information Master 10A

3 **Developing Vocabulary:** After discussing the New Ideas—*need* and *want*—in this Preview, reinforce them as they arise in the text.

Problem Solving Groupwork

Phase 1: Exploring Families' Everyday Needs and Wants

1 **Prepare materials for Needs and Wants Bingo.** Cut the cards from *Information Master 10B: Bingo Cards.* Put them aside for use with the game in Step 5.

2 **Read about families' needs and wants.** Read aloud Sections 10.1–10.4 in the *Social Studies Alive! My School and Family* Student Edition as students follow along.

3 **Find evidence showing how a family meets its needs and wants.** After reading, project *Transparency 10A: What Do Families Need and Want?*

- Ask students to name all the objects and activities in the illustration that show how this family meets their needs for food, for clothing, and for shelter. (**Note:** You may need to briefly discuss what it means to "meet" a need.) In discussing the need for shelter, help students understand that shelter encompasses more than just the buildings people live in; it includes the furnishings they need (beds, bedding, tables, chairs) as well as lighting and heating or air conditioning.

- Ask students to name the objects and activities that show things this family has bought to meet their wants.

- Discuss the idea that in addition to selling *goods* that meet our needs and wants, some people in a community offer *services* to meet our needs and wants—in other words, things we need and want that other people do for us. Brainstorm with students a few such services (e.g., haircuts, health care, fire fighting, mail delivery, garbage pickup, car repair, banking, day care).

4 **Have students show what they have learned about needs and wants.** Ask them to turn to Reading Notes 10 in their Interactive Student Notebooks. Read the directions aloud and have students complete the page, filling the nine boxes with different needs and wants. Tell students that they are making a bingo board for a game they will be playing on another day. Remind them to label each drawing as a need or a want, as that will be important in the game.

5 **Have students review needs and wants by playing *Needs and Wants Bingo.*** Put students into mixed-ability pairs, and give each pair several bingo markers (counters, buttons, or similar items).

- Have students again open their Interactive Student Notebooks to Reading Notes 10. Explain that they will use the drawings they made to play a game of bingo. Help pairs choose one of their bingo boards to use for the first game.

- Tell students you will randomly choose a card (from Information Master 10B) and read it aloud. You will read a number and either *Need* or *Want.* If you read "4 Want," any pair who drew a want in Box 4 should put a marker on that box.

Information Master 10B

Transparency 10A

- When a pair has placed three markers in a row—down, across, or corner to corner—that pair calls out "Bingo." Ask the players to tell you what wants and needs they drew in the covered row. Check the winning board to see that the players' markers match the cards you have read.

- Play the game again, this time with pairs using the other student's game board.

Phase 2: Identifying Needs and Wants Away from Home

6 **Prepare a simple camping triarama to serve as a model.** Follow the directions on *Information Master 10C: How to Make a Triarama.* You can either include fold-over tabs at the bottom of each stage prop, gluing them to make a stand-up scene, or simply glue these items to the sides and floor of the triarama.

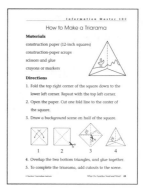

Information Master 10C

7 **Use a team-builder exercise to help groups feel comfortable working together.** Put students into mixed-ability groups of three. Tell them to think about the best family vacation ever. Then have them share their ideas with their groups.

8 **Introduce the idea of camping.** Keep in mind that many students may not have experienced camping.

- Project *Transparency 10B: Camping Shelter.* Ask: *Where is this family? What do you think they are doing?* If any students have been camping, have them share their experiences. (**Note:** It does not matter if students have never been camping. The point is for them to engage in critical thinking about the things they would need and want while away from home.)

Transparencies 10B–10D

- Explain that when families go camping, they leave home and go somewhere outdoors, such as the woods, to live for a short time. Ask: *Do families still need food, clothing, and shelter when they go camping? What need is the family in this picture trying to meet? How would you use a tent for camping?*

- Project *Transparency 10C: Camping Food.* Ask: *Where is this family? What are they doing?* Explain that this family is also on a camping trip. Ask: *What food might they be cooking? What are they using to cook their food? When you eat food at home, how does your family cook it? Would you have a stove or an oven if you were camping?*

- Project *Transparency 10D: Camping Clothing.* Ask: *What are the people wearing? Why are they wearing this type of clothing?* Explain that some families like to camp in places where the air can be very cold, especially after the sun sets. These people are wearing clothes that keep them warm. Besides warm clothing, they will also need warm sleeping bags.

9 **Tell students that they will be deciding what things they would need and want for a vacation outdoors, a long way from home.**

- Explain that each group will plan a family camping trip in the mountains, in the woods, or at the beach. Project *Transparencies 10E–10G: Camping Places.* Point out that there are no houses in these pictures, so students will have to bring everything they need for staying outdoors overnight.

Transparencies 10E–10G

- Help students name things they have at home that they would miss if they went camping. For example, at home, they can switch on a light when it's dark, but there will be no light switch outdoors. What could they take with them for lighting? Continue with similar suggestions (bedding, stove, refrigerator, food, dishes) until students seem prepared to identify their needs and wants for a camping trip.

- Randomly distribute *Placards 10A–10C: Camping Places,* one to each group. Explain that each group will make a triarama showing their plans to go camping in the place shown on their placard. They will include pictures of the objects they decide to bring with them to meet their needs and wants. Show your model and briefly explain how you made it.

Placards 10A–10C

10 Help students understand their individual roles within their group.

- Project a transparency of *Information Master 10D: Roles for Your Group.* Explain the three roles: Artist, Writer, and Presenter. Assign a role to each group member.

- Distribute a copy of *Student Handout 10: Planning a Camping Triarama* to each group. Explain that groups will use these two sheets to help plan their triaramas. Tell them to choose three kinds of food, three kinds of clothing, and three kinds of shelter they need for their camping trip, plus three wants they'd like to take on the trip. The Writer will write down the group's choices.

Information Master 10D

- Explain that groups will choose just one item each of food, clothing, and shelter to make out of construction paper. (**Note:** They are not expected to select the most important need, just the one they would like to illustrate.) The Writer will circle their choices. They will make representations of all three wants they have listed.

11 Have groups complete Student Handout 10 to plan the needs and wants they will show in their triaramas. Stop the activity when students have finished planning their triaramas. Continue with Step 11 another day. (**Note:** Do not expect that the students' choices for camping will always be realistic. The goal is that they be able to distinguish between their needs and their wants for a trip away from home.)

12 Have groups create their camping triaramas. Students continue working in their same groups of three.

- Project a transparency of Information Master 10C as you explain how groups will construct their triaramas. Show students where the construction materials are.

Student Handout 10

- Point out that the Artist will color the background on the top two triangles, above the cut. The Artist may want to look at the group's placard for ideas.

- Demonstrate how to cut and glue the triarama structure, after the background is complete.

- Use your model triarama to point out how you have added needs and wants to the scene. Project the transparency of Information Master 10D again to review the group roles. Explain that the Writer and the Presenter can work on their needs and wants while the Artist is coloring the background for their scene.

- Give groups plenty of time to create the background, make their add-on pictures, and glue them into place.

13 **Have groups display their triaramas on their desks.** Explain that the Presenter for each group will stand and talk about their triarama's background and the three needs and three wants the group made. Remind the class to be attentive while each Presenter takes a turn.

Reading Further: Meeting Wants and Needs

1 **Introduce the idea that families need money to pay for their needs and wants.** Ask students for their ideas about how families generally get that money. Help them understand that one or more adults in the family typically work at jobs. They are paid money for the work they do. Ask: *What are some jobs that people do to earn money?*

2 **Project *Transparency 10H: The Farmer's Field*.** Ask:

- What do you see in this picture?

- What is the man doing? Where do you think he is?

- What kind of plants do you think these are? What do you think will happen to the plants?

- What do you think this man's job is?

3 **Explain that this man's job is farming, and this is a picture of a crop he has planted.** Ask: *How do you think a farmer earns money to meet his family's needs?*

4 **Open the Big Book to Reading Further 10 and read it aloud while students follow along.** As you read, pause on each page to help students identify and discuss the jobs of the various workers referred to in the text and shown in the illustrations. Help students understand that all these jobs are ways to earn money to pay for a family's needs and wants. Briefly introduce the terms *producers* and *consumers*. Help students distinguish between the two but also recognize that the same person can be both a producer (while working on his or her job) and a consumer (while buying things at a store to meet the family's needs).

5 **Build students' sequencing skills.** Ask students to rise to the challenge of the last paragraph and retell the story, in sequence, of how popcorn gets from the field to the bowl.

- Have students open their Interactive Student Notebooks to Reading Further 10. Read the directions and give students time to draw, in order, at least four of the workers involved in the production and sale of popcorn.

Transparency 10H

Reading Strategy: Use Context Clues

Before reading, sketch on the board a green, leafy plant and a grain processing plant (e.g., long building, tall silos for grain storage). Write the word *plant* and discuss both meanings. Explain that when we read a word like this in a story, we can use context clues—including the rest of the sentence and pictures on the page—to decide which meaning is meant. Reinforce this idea when you read about the *plant* and *plant workers*.

- Call on students one at a time to name the steps and the workers involved in each step. List their steps on the board in the order mentioned.

- When students believe they have the correct sequence, have them look at their Student Editions to confirm the process. Ask them to see if any steps are missing from their sequence.

Processing

1 **Have groups display their triaramas again.**

2 **Review the concepts of needs and wants.** Replay CD Track 9 and have students sing along. Ask: *What is a want? What is a need?*

3 **Have students open to Processing 10 in their Interactive Student Notebooks.** Read and model the directions. Explain that students will walk around the room to find one need and one want—other than their own group's needs and wants—that they really like.

4 **Conduct a "gallery walk."** Assign half of the groups to walk around the room, viewing the triaramas. Students can ask questions about the triaramas as they search for their favorite need and want. Then switch groups.

5 **Have students complete Processing 10.** Explain that after they draw and label one camping need and one camping want that they really liked, they should complete each sentence to justify why one is a need and the other is a want.

Assessment

Masters for the chapter assessment appear in the *Lesson Masters*.
Answers appear below.

Big Ideas

1. green circles: sandwich, house, shoes

2. red circles: TV, toy

3. circle: farm worker

Show You Know

4. The bulleted points can serve as a rubric for this item.

English Language Learners

When students make their triaramas during Phase 2 of the Problem Solving Groupwork activity, appoint English Language Learners to be the Artists in their groups so that they can take ownership of an important role yet not be frustrated by the language component.

Students with Special Needs

Before the gallery walk at the end of the lesson, provide students with sample questions that they might ask the Presenters. Then as students work on Processing 10 in their Interactive Student Notebooks, assist them with the labeling and sentence completion that accompanies their pictures. They can trace over your lettering or copy what you write, as appropriate.

Enrichment

Enlist student help in setting up a simulated grocery store. Distribute index cards and have mixed-ability pairs use these to draw and label individual grocery items for sale. You might provide grocery flyers as a source of ideas. Assign a simple price to each item. Ask for volunteers to perform the service jobs in the store—stock clerks, store manager, cashiers, baggers. Put the managers and stock clerks in charge of arranging the grocery items in general categories on a table or other surface. Give each remaining pair a fixed amount of play dollars to "buy groceries" for their family. When they have spent their money, have them write a short "shopping report" listing what they bought and labeling each item a need or a want. Have students take turns working in the store so that service workers also have a chance to shop.

Enrichment Resources

Have students find out more about families' wants and needs by exploring the following Enrichment Resources for *Social Studies Alive! My School and Family,* at www.learntci.com.

Internet Connections

These recommended Web sites provide useful and engaging content that enforces skills development and mastery of subjects within the chapter.

Enrichment Readings

These in-depth readings encourage students to explore selected topics related to the chapter. For Chapter 10, you may wish to use one or more of the Enrichment Readings listed for the chapter. You may also find readings that relate the chapter's content directly to your state's curriculum.

Additional Reading Opportunities

These books, which can be read aloud to students, offer opportunities to extend the content in this chapter.

If You Give a Pig a Pancake by Laura Joffe Numeroff. Illustrated by Felicia Bond. (New York: HarperCollins, 1998)

This sequel to two similar, well-known titles about a mouse and a moose, created by the same author–illustrator team, offers more chances for students to distinguish between *wants* and *needs*. This series offers a model for student-created stories: "If you give a kid a sleeping bag, chances are he'll want…"

Stella and Roy Go Camping by Ashley Wolff (El Portal, CA: Yosemite Association, 2006)

For children unfamiliar with camping, this story of a family camping trip in the mountains reveals many of the details involved. Even if the setting is unfamiliar, students will relate to the rivalry between the boy who keeps pointing out "bear" tracks and the older sister who is quick to correct him with her animal field guide—until the time she is wrong.

Tight Times by Barbara Shook Hazen. Illustrated by Trina Schart Hyman. (New York: Puffin Books, 1987)

When a family has financial troubles, their little boy has to learn the difference between *needs* and *wants*. Strong family bonds offer reassurance during hard times.

Draw a need in five boxes.

Draw a want in four boxes.

Label each drawing "need" or "want."

NEEDS AND WANTS BINGO		
1 Answers will vary. Needs might include a home, basic furnishings, basic clothing, and healthy foods. Wants might include toys, snack foods, and other nonessentials.	**2**	**3**
4	**5**	**6**
7	**8**	**9**

How Do Family Members Care for Each Other?

Overview

Students learn about ways family members care for each other. In the Preview activity, students think about things they do at home to help their families meet three categories of family needs. In a Response Group activity, they sort family pictures into three categories of caring for each other—helping each other, sharing knowledge, and spending time together. In the Reading Further, they learn ways that children in schools can take care of the Earth. In the Processing activity, students write Proclamation Scrolls to list ways they intend to help their families or show that they care.

Objectives

Social Studies

- Sort pictures of family activities into three categories of caring and explain the sorting decisions.
- Give examples of one's own family activities to relate new concepts to personal experience.
- Identify a local problem related to Earth and its resources, and make a plan for solving the problem.

Language Arts

- Present reasons for a choice and challenge or support others' choices. (speaking and listening)
- Do prewriting and writing to create a scroll. (writing)

Social Studies Vocabulary

help each other, share what you know, spend time together

Materials

Social Studies Alive! My School and Family Big Book and Student Editions

Transparencies 11A and 11B

Placards 11A–11F

Interactive Student Notebooks

Lesson Masters

- Student Handouts 11A–11E

envelopes

chart paper

Time Estimates

Preview: 30 min.

Response Group: 4 sessions (30 min. each)

Reading Further: 30 min.

Processing: 30 min.

Activity	Suggested Time	Materials
Preview • Connecting to Prior Knowledge • Developing Vocabulary • Building Background Knowledge	30 minutes	• *Social Studies Alive! My School and Family* Big Book, Chapter 11 • Transparency 11A • Interactive Student Notebooks • chart paper
Response Group Sorting family pictures into three ways of caring, and explaining the group's choices	30-minute sessions (4) • Categorizing pictures (Steps 1–5) • Explaining the choices (Steps 6–8) • Learning more about family chores and sharing (Steps 9–11) • Learning more about family feelings and activities (Steps 12–14)	• *Social Studies Alive! My School and Family* Student Editions, Sections 11.1–11.4 • Placards 11A–11F • Interactive Student Notebooks • Student Handout 11A (1 copy per group of 3, cut apart and placed in an envelope) • Student Handouts 11B–11D (1 set per group of 3)
Reading Further Learning ways that children can help in caring for the Earth, just as they do for their families	30 minutes	• *Social Studies Alive! My School and Family* Student Editions, Chapter 11 Reading Further • Transparency 11B • Interactive Student Notebooks
Processing Creating a scroll that identifies ways to help one's family	30 minutes	• Interactive Student Notebooks • Student Handout 11E (1 per student)
Assessment	15 minutes	• Chapter 11 Assessment, Lesson Masters • Chapter 11 Assessment, Digital Teacher Resources

Preview

1 **Connecting to Prior Knowledge:** Before class, set up three columns on chart paper to review how we can categorize concepts, as presented in Chapter 10.

- For a review of a family's basic needs, have students turn to Preview 11 in their Interactive Student Notebooks. Read the directions and questions aloud. Have students identify, with words and pictures, three family needs. When students have finished their work, ask for volunteers to share their answers. Write the answers (*Food, Clothing, Home or Shelter*) and draw a picture symbol for each one; these will be the three column headings for the chart.

- Fill in the columns of the chart one by one to help students practice thinking in categories. Ask them what they help their families do to meet the needs for food, clothing, and a home. Draw a simple symbol as a visual cue for each idea (for example, draw a table for *set the table*).

- When the chart is complete, point out that it shows many ways the students help their families in three different categories. Let them know that in this lesson, they will learn about other ways family members help and care for each other.

2 **Developing Vocabulary:** Cover New Ideas—*help each other, share what you know,* and *spend time together*—as they arise in the text. You may want to discuss some terms before beginning the activity, using methods described in *Solutions for Effective Instruction.*

3 **Building Background Knowledge:** Help students identify some ways family members help and care for each other.

- Turn through Chapter 11 in the *Social Studies Alive! My School and Family* Big Book, reading just the section titles aloud. Ask students how each picture shows something that the section title talks about.

- Project *Transparency 11A: How Do Family Members Care for Each Other?* As students view the illustration, ask: *Where do you see family members helping each other? Where are family members sharing what they know? Where are family members spending time together?* (**Note:** Expect students to mention the same illustrated situations to answer more than one of these questions. This will help prepare them for the type of critical thinking they will be doing in the Response Group activity.)

Transparency 11A

Response Group

1 **Prepare materials for the activity.** For each group of three students, cut the six pictures from a copy of *Student Handout 11A: Family Pictures* and put them in an envelope. Copy *Student Handouts 11B–11D: Circles* for each group. Draw three large circles on the board, each large enough for taping two or three placards inside. Label these circles to match the labels on Student Handouts 11B–11D.

2 **Remind students of the Response Group guidelines.** Put students in mixed-ability groups of three and choose one student in each group to be the Presenter. Review the Response Group guidelines:

- Sit cross-legged with knees touching.

- Give everyone a chance to talk.

- Listen to others when they talk.

- When the group is done talking, straighten your legs out in front of you.

3 **Conduct a team builder that gets students talking about ways they care for their family members.** Tell students that you want each of them to share one way that they care for people in their family. Remind groups to signal you when they have finished sharing.

4 **Introduce three categories of how family members care for each other.**

- Point to the three circles on the board, and read each heading. Remind students that these are ways family members care for each other.

- Give Student Handouts 11B–11D to each group. Point out that these circles have the same headings as those on the board.

- Give each group an envelope containing the pictures from Student Handout 11A.

- Ask groups to spread the pictures out in front of them. Explain that these are pictures of family members caring for each other in different ways. Tell students that each group will talk together to choose the circle that is the best category for each picture. When they have decided, they should glue the pictures into the chosen circles. Before they begin, review the meaning of each heading once again. (**Note:** These pictures are intentionally ambiguous to promote discussion of the concepts. Each picture can be interpreted as representing more than one category.)

5 **Have groups sort their six family pictures into the three categories.** Remind students to signal you when their group has finished.

6 **Prepare materials for the class discussion of the results of the group sorting.** Put a few loops of tape on the back of each of *Placards 11A–11F: Family Pictures.* Place the six placards along the chalk rail.

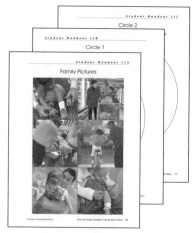

Student Handouts 11A–11D

Vocabulary Development: Make Picture-Sentence Cards

For the Response Group work, students need to be able to read the three category headings and understand the meaning of each one. On half sheets of paper, have students write each heading as a sentence and then draw a picture to illustrate that category. They can use the cards for reference in their groups.

Placards 11A–11F

7 Ask groups to share their sorting results, encouraging different points of view for a lively class discussion.

- Ask a volunteer Presenter to place the first placard in the circle where his or her group thinks it belongs. Let the class know that there is not one correct answer; different groups will have different answers. Ask the volunteer to explain why his or her group chose that circle for that picture.

- Ask the other groups whether they chose the same circle. You may wish to call on each Presenter to explain his or her group's choice of circle for that placard, and then let other students comment. Use this discussion to point out again that family members help and care for each other in many ways.

8 Repeat Step 7 for the remaining five placards.

9 Read to reinforce the ways that families help each other at home. Read aloud Section 11.1 in the *Social Studies Alive! My School and Family* Student Edition as students follow along in their books. Then ask:

- How do the adults in your home help with chores?
- How do the children in your home help with chores?
- Who in your family makes the rules about chores?
- Which chores are your responsibility?

10 Read to reinforce the ways that families share what they know. Read aloud Section 11.2 as students follow along in their books. Then ask:

- How do the adults in your home share what they know?
- How do the children in your home share what they know?
- What knowledge do you share with your family?

11 Have students relate the reading to their personal experience. Ask them to turn to Reading Notes 11 in their Interactive Student Notebooks. Read aloud the directions for Part A and have students complete the page.

12 Read about and discuss the ways families show their feelings. Read aloud Section 11.3 as students follow along. Then ask:

- How do you show that you care about the members of your family?
- Why is showing your feelings important?

13 Read to review the things that family members do together. Read aloud Section 11.4 and the Summary as students follow along. Then ask:

- How do the people in your family spend time together?
- What is your favorite thing to do with your family?
- Are there things you do as a family that not everyone enjoys?

Help students understand that we sometimes do things with our families that we don't especially enjoy, simply because spending time together is important to the family group. That is, participating in family activities is our responsibility.

14 Have students complete Part B of Reading Notes 11.

> **Reading Strategy:**
> **Find Supporting Details**
>
> Show students how they can use a graphic organizer, such as a web, to map the information presented in each section. Have them find the main idea in the section title (in this case, *help each other*) and write it in the center of the web. Then have them identify supporting details that tell more about the main idea. Show students how to write these on spurs around the web's center. Have them create similar webs for each section of the text.

Reading Further: Taking Care of Earth

1   **Project** *Transparency 11B: Taking Care of Earth*. Ask the following visual discovery questions to help students make some predictions about the story.

Transparency 11B

- What do you see in this picture?

- Who do you think made these posters?

- Are the posters about taking care of people in our families? What do you think the posters are telling us?

2   **Turn to Reading Further 11 in the Big Book.** Read it aloud while students follow along in their Student Editions. Pause during the reading to ask the following questions:

- Who knows the purpose of Earth Day?

- When the children at Park School talk about a "green" school, do they mean a school painted the color green? What do they mean?

3   **Help students understand how the plan made by each grade at Park School is tied to our use of Earth's natural resources.** Point out that just as a family provides for our basic needs, the Earth provides land, air, and water to meet the needs of everyone around the world. As needed, provide additional information such as the following.

- *Park School, Grade 1:* Water is a precious resource that is in short supply in many parts of the world. Everyone needs water for drinking, cooking, and keeping clean. We get water from streams, rivers, and lakes, or from under the ground. When we let it leak on the ground, or when we leave the water running when we aren't using it, we are being wasteful.

- *Park School, Grade 2:* One of the ways we get electricity is by burning fuels such as coal, oil, and natural gas in power plants. This uses up natural resources that can never be replaced. These kinds of power plants also contribute to air pollution. If we can find ways to use less electricity, or power, we are helping to save both fuel and the air we breathe. We can also help by placing solar panels on our roofs; these panels turn energy from the sun into electric power.

- *Park School, Grade 3:* Trees play an important role in keeping the air clean so that people and animals have the oxygen they need to live. Trees provide shade to cool our homes. In addition, many animals and birds depend on trees for their homes and for food.

- *Park School, Grade 4:* Too much trash shows that resources are being wasted. We can recycle or reduce the use of paper, glass, cans, and plastics. We can also make compost from discarded plant material and certain food scraps, and then add the compost to garden soil. All these ideas can help save trees, oil, energy, water, and landfill space.

4   **Help students identify a problem related to the use of natural resources in their own school or community.** Work with them to analyze the problem and ask them to suggest solutions.

- While selecting a problem or possible solutions, poll the students on the options they would like to pursue as a class. Write three or four choices across the board and have students line up in front of the one they prefer, making a human bar graph. Write numbers on the board to reflect the results. (**Option:** Have students create graphs on paper to show the results of their vote, using an X or a small box for each student. If students have limited experience with graphing, model this on the board.)

- Once students decide on a plan, help them formulate it as a class pledge (similar to the one they will make to their family in the Processing activity): "We, (class identifier), will take care of Earth by . . ." Possible ideas:

  Collection and sorting of non-food trash: What could students do to reduce this amount of trash?

  Reduction of school-wide paper use: What could students do to encourage this?

  See the Internet Connections for this chapter for further project ideas.

5   **Point out how the class plan fits into the larger picture of environmentalism.** Students may well identify a problem that they cannot solve on an individual or class basis. Reinforce the idea, introduced in the story "Taking Care of Earth," that even though we cannot fix everything with one action, we can attack the problem by taking small steps, day after day. Help students understand that their responsibility is simply to act as if "every day is Earth Day" and to do whatever they can to save natural resources.

6   **Have students plan posters that explain their ideas for solving the school or community problem they have identified.** Pair students to complete Reading Further 11 in their Interactive Student Notebooks. Encourage partners to talk about a possible animal character they could use to help promote their ideas, similar to Smokey Bear, the character who raises public awareness about preventing forest fires. (**Note:** Creating larger posters from students' plans is optional, depending on the time you want to allot to this activity.)

Processing

1 **Prepare materials for the Proclamation Scrolls.** Make one copy of *Student Handout 11E: Proclamation Scroll* for each student. Create a sample scroll by writing a simple sentence and decorating the scroll.

2 **Dramatically present and read your scroll to the class.** Tell students that they will make a similar Proclamation Scroll to present to their families. Explain that a *proclamation* is a statement that someone makes in public to tell everyone what that person plans to do.

3 **Have students do some prewriting brainstorming work.** Have them turn to Processing 11 in their Interactive Student Notebooks. Read aloud the three questions. After students have written or drawn some of their ideas, ask for volunteers to share. During this sharing, create a word bank on the board, writing words and phrases that students might need for their scrolls.

4 **Have students create their scrolls.** Distribute Student Handout 11E. Ask students to look at their brainstorming work and choose one way they want to help their families. Explain that they will write or dictate a sentence about how they will help. Finally, they will decorate their scrolls. Check their work when they have finished.

5 **Give students time to practice presenting their scrolls to their families.** Have pairs of students meet at the Sharing Spot, a place in the room where students can quietly read to each other, and practice reading their scrolls before taking them home for presentation. Show students how to roll their scrolls loosely so they can unroll them for dramatic effect.

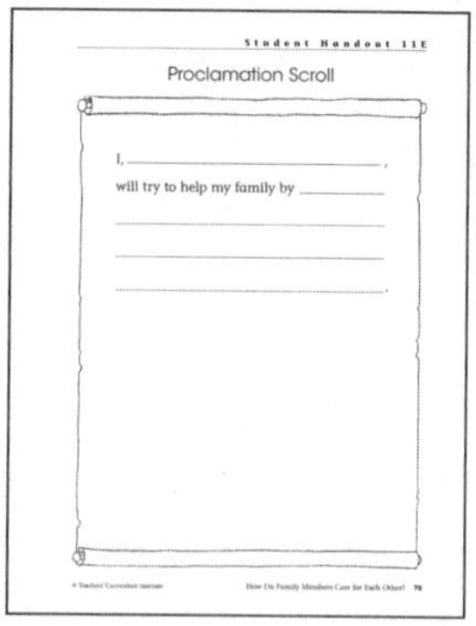

Student Handout 11E

Assessment

Masters for the chapter assessment appear in the *Lesson Masters*. Answers appear below.

Big Ideas

1. Answers will vary. Sample answer: blue circle around either woman or man helping child learn to ride a bicycle

2. Answers will vary. Sample answers: red circle around father and child on bridge; red circle around boy with arm around other boy's shoulders

3. color green: child planting a tree

Show You Know

4. The picture and sentence can serve as a two-point rubric for this item.

English Language Learners

In the Processing activity, as students create their Proclamation Scrolls, allow them to draw what they would like to do and dictate their sentences, which they can then copy or trace. Have them practice reading the English words aloud, but encourage them to deliver their proclamations to their family members in both English and their first language to facilitate greater family discussions of the concepts at home.

Students with Special Needs

During the Response Group activity, have students act out or role-play ideas for each of the categories (*helping each other, sharing what you know, spending time together*). By creating bodily-kinesthetic associations to the verbal and visual cues discussed in class, students will be better able to make connections and retain the concepts.

Enrichment

In conjunction with the Reading Further activity, have students work on a school-wide plan similar to the one made by the students at Park School. For example, if the students pledge to reduce the amount of trash in the school, have them deliver their pledge to one class at each grade in your school. After sharing their own pledges, students can provide ideas that might encourage second, third, or fourth graders to contribute to the plan. Students can then report back how the classes at the other grades will support the idea of "greening" your school.

Enrichment Resources

Have students find out more about how families care for each other and for the environment by exploring the following Enrichment Resources for *Social Studies Alive! My School and Family,* at www.learntci.com.

Internet Connections

These recommended Web sites provide useful and engaging content that enforces skills development and mastery of subjects within the chapter.

Enrichment Readings

These in-depth readings encourage students to explore selected topics related to the chapter. For Chapter 11, you may wish to use one or more of the Enrichment Readings listed for the chapter. You may also find readings that relate the chapter's content directly to your state's curriculum.

Additional Reading Opportunities

These fiction and nonfiction books, which can be read aloud to students, offer opportunities to extend the content in this chapter.

In My Heart by Molly Bang (New York: Little, Brown Books for Young Readers, 2006)

Colorful illustrations with a multicultural cast of characters show students how families care for each other.

Recycle Every Day! by Nancy Elizabeth Wallace (Tarrytown, NY: Marshall Cavendish Children's Books, 2006)

Minna the bunny is working on a recycling poster for a school contest. She gets ideas as her family tries composting, taking old clothes to the clothing bank, crushing cans, using cloth shopping bags, and more.

Smack Dab in the Middle by Anita Riggio (New York: Putnam, 2002)

In Rosie's extended family of 29 people, she often feels unappreciated and jealous of her siblings. A teacher helps Rosie discover that her family does care for her, even though they may not show it in the ways she expects.

Why Are the Ice Caps Melting? The Dangers of Global Warming by Anne Rockwell. Illustrated by Paul Meisel. (New York: Collins, 2006)

Easy-to-understand text helps students to understand this important topic and offers some simple ideas for countering the trend.

How Do Families Change?

Overview

Students learn about ways families change over time. In the Preview activity, students think about changes they have seen in their own families. In a Visual Discovery activity, they explore what happens when people grow older. They also learn some reasons why families change in size. In Reading Further, students see that old photographs can show changes in the ways families work and play. In the Processing activity, students apply what they have learned by illustrating ways they expect their own families to change in the future.

Objectives

Social Studies

- Identify three ways in which families change over time.
- Name responsibilities and activities that change as a child grows older.
- Identify at least two reasons for changes in family size.
- Compare old and new ways of doing work.
- Predict future changes in a family.

Language Arts

- Gather information aurally. (speaking and listening)
- Use transition words to indicate sequence. (writing)

Social Studies Vocabulary

change, grow, move

Materials

*Social Studies Alive!
My School and Family*
Big Book and Student
Editions

Transparencies 12A–12D

Interactive Student
Notebooks

Lesson Masters
- Information Masters
  12A and 12B
- Student Handouts
  12A and 12B

CD Track 10

Time Estimates

Preview: 20 min.

Visual Discovery:
2 sessions (20 min. each)

Reading Further: 25 min.

Processing: 20 min.

Activity	Suggested Time	Materials
Preview • Connecting to Prior Knowledge • Building Background Knowledge • Developing Vocabulary	20 minutes	• *Social Studies Alive! My School and Family* Big Book, Chapter 12 • Interactive Student Notebooks • Information Master 12A • CD Track 10
Visual Discovery Discovering how families change over time	20-minute sessions (2) • Learning how families change as people grow older (Steps 1–4) • Learning ways that families change in size (Steps 5–10)	• *Social Studies Alive! My School and Family* Big Book and Student Editions, Sections 12.1–12.4 • Transparencies 12A–12C • Interactive Student Notebooks • Information Master 12B • Student Handout 12A (1 per student, plus 1 extra)
Reading Further Seeing changes in styles and ways of life over time	25 minutes	• *Social Studies Alive! My School and Family* Big Book and Student Editions, Chapter 12 Reading Further • Transparency 12D • Interactive Student Notebooks
Processing Making predictions about how one's family will change	20 minutes	• Interactive Student Notebooks • Student Handout 12B (1 per student, plus 1 extra) • Processing 12 (1 transparency, made from the Interactive Student Notebook page)
Assessment	15 minutes	• Chapter 12 Assessment, Lesson Masters • Chapter 12 Assessment, Digital Teacher Resources

Preview

1 Connecting to Prior Knowledge: Prepare students to understand the variety of ways in which families change over time.

- Help students think about the passage of time in their own lives. Ask: *For as far back as you can remember, has your family always been the same? Has it always had the same number of people? Have you always lived in the same place? What about you—have you changed? Have you always been the same size? How do you know?*

- Have students open their Interactive Student Notebooks to Preview 12. Read the directions aloud. Have students write about and illustrate one change that they have seen in their family. Remind them that this could include a change in themselves.

2 Building Background Knowledge: Use a song to introduce three ways that families change over time.

- Play CD Track 10, "Families Change." Project a transparency of the lyrics on *Information Master 12A: Families Change* so that students can follow along.

- Ask students to listen for three ways that families change as you play the song again. Help students recall the three ways mentioned in the song, and write them on the board or highlight relevant words on the lyrics transparency. *(grow older, grow bigger, move away)*

- Play the song a third time, and ask students to sing along.

- To reinforce the new ideas, turn to Chapter 12 in *Social Studies Alive! My School and Family* Big Book. Read aloud Sections 12.1–12.4. Have volunteers answer the question at the end of each section.

3 Developing Vocabulary: Cover New Ideas—*change, grow,* and *move*—as they arise in the text. You may want to discuss some terms before beginning the activity, using methods described in *Solutions for Effective Instruction*.

Information Master 12A

Visual Discovery

1 Project *Transparency 12A: A Young Family* to introduce the relationship between age and responsibilities. Ask questions such as:

- What would you call the different members of this family? *(mother, father, little brother, big sister)*

- How old might the girl be? *(about 7)*

- How old might the boy be? *(about 5)*

- Do you think the children are allowed to walk to school by themselves? Stay up until midnight? Drive a car? Why or why not? *(No; they are too young.)*

- What chores do you think the girl might do after school to help her family? *(feed the dog, and so on)*

- What chores might the boy do? *(set the table, and so on)*

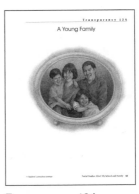

Transparency 12A

2 **Project *Transparency 12B: A Family Grows Older* to explore family changes over time.** Ask questions such as:

- What do you see? Do these new pictures show the same family? What makes you think so?

- How old do you think the children are now? *(about 13 and 11)*

- What is different about the mother? *(longer hair, job)* The father? *(a little gray hair)* The girl? The boy? *(both look and act older)*

- What chores might the girl do now? *(walk the dog, help fix dinner/do laundry, and so on)*

- What chores might the boy do now? *(weed the garden, help fix dinner/do laundry, and so on)*

- What might they be allowed to do now that they are older? *(stay up later, walk to school with friends, and so on)*

    Point out that things change as children grow older, including the way they look, their chores around the house, and the things they are allowed to do.

3 **To review the changes that happen as people age, read Sections 12.1 and 12.2 in the Big Book.** Ask students to follow along in their Student Editions. Call on volunteers to answer the question at the end of each section.

4 **Ask students to identify changes that come with growing older.** Have them open their Interactive Student Notebooks to Reading Notes 12, Part A. Read the directions aloud, and have students complete the page, identifying chores and privileges they expect to have when they are older.

5 **To explore some ways that families change in size, display *Transparency 12C: Ted's Changing Family*.** Distribute *Student Handout 12A: Ted's Changing Family* and three crayons (blue, red, and green) to each student. Point out that the picture on the handout is the same as the colorful one on the transparency. Tell students that you will read a story. They must listen carefully to decide who everyone in the picture is, and follow the directions they hear.

6 **Read aloud the story on *Information Master 12B: Ted's Story*.** Pause at each instruction in bold type, giving students time to locate the individuals.

7 **Debrief the activity, asking students to describe the ways that Ted's family has grown.** Keep Transparency 12C projected and ask these questions:

- Who has blue circles around them? *(Grandma, Mom, Dad)*

- How did Ted come to be in his family? *(He was born.)*

- Who has red circles? *(Meg and Sam)*

- How did these two come to be in Ted's family? *(They are the children of Ted's father and his first wife, before he married Ted's mother.)*

- Who has a green circle? *(baby Brad)*

- How did the new baby come to be in Ted's family? *(Ted's parents adopted him.)*

Transparencies 12B and 12C

Student Handout 12A

Information Master 12B

Speaking and Listening: Match Spoken Clues to Pictures

As you read Ted's story, stop after introducing each new character. Call on a volunteer to point out that person on Transparency 12C. Ask that student which words in the story helped locate the right person in the picture.

8 Help students summarize and sequence the growth of Ted's family.

- As students tell you what happened, write these three steps on the board, using transition words: First, Ted's dad and mom got married. Next, Ted was born. Later, the family adopted a baby.

- Point out that Ted's family grew bigger in three ways: by marriage, birth, and adoption. If students are curious, you may want to further explore the meaning of adoption, perhaps using a read-aloud picture book from the Additional Reading Opportunities for Chapter 12.

9 Review ways that families can change in size by reading aloud Sections 12.3 and 12.4 in the Big Book. Have students follow along in their Student Editions. After reading Section 12.3, ask:

- What are some reasons families grow bigger?

- Has your family grown bigger? How?

After reading Section 12.4, ask:

- What are some reasons people move to new places?

- Has your family moved to a new neighborhood or home? Why did your family move?

10 Have students identify at least two ways that families can change in size. Have them turn to Reading Notes 12, Part B, in their Interactive Student Notebooks. Read the directions aloud and have students complete the page. Allow them to refer to their copies of Student Handout 12A, where they have circled members of Ted's family, if this helps them remember the details.

> **Writing Tip:**
> **Use Transition Words**
> Write the transition words *first, next, then,* and *later* on the board. As students complete Reading Notes 12, Part B, encourage them to use some of these words in their sentences that tell how Ted's family changed.

Reading Further: Old Family Pictures

1 Introduce students to one way that the changes in technology have changed family life. Project *Transparency 12D: Changing Ways of Life* and ask the following questions:

- What do you see in this picture?

- Do you think this is a picture from today or from long ago? What makes you think so?

- What do you think the woman is doing?

- Do your parents do anything like this? How is what they do different from this?

- Which way do you think is easier? Why?

Transparency 12D

2 **Explain that this is one of the photographs they will see in the story "Old Family Pictures."**

- If students are able to identify this as a washing machine, you might spend some time with them talking about how the wringer worked, and why it was needed. Compare it to the spin cycle in modern washers.

- Then ask students if they have ever looked at old family photographs. If they have, ask: *What did you notice? Do the people look different from people today? In what ways? What else in the photos looks different to you?*

3 **Open the Big Book to Reading Further 12 and read it aloud while students follow along.**

- Discuss point of view. Point out that the story says, "I like to spend time at Grandma's house." Help them identify as the speaker the boy in the photograph, who is about their age.

- As you read, pause to ask students how each situation is different from the life they know today. They should notice clothing styles as well as differences in the tools and appliances people are using. Point out that when their grandparents and great-grandparents were raising their families, many mothers stayed home to do the housework, while the fathers usually worked at jobs outside the home. Discuss how that is different from today.

4 **Help students recognize more ways that technology in the home has changed over time.** Have them open their Interactive Student Notebooks to Reading Further 12. Read the directions aloud, and have students describe the images on the page. Be sure they understand what each image shows (washing machine, typewriter, telephone) before they draw its modern counterpart.

5 **Conclude this activity with some pantomime.** Start by dramatically going through the motions suggested by each picture from long ago: running wet clothes through a wringer and catching them on the other side; inserting the paper into a manual typewriter, typing and hitting the carriage return at the end of a line; dialing a phone number. Have students join you in each pantomime. Then ask volunteers to pantomime the use of the modern equivalents. Ask: *What is different about the things we use today? What is the same?*

Processing

1 **Have students apply what they have learned by predicting future changes in their own families.** Have students open to Processing 12 in their Interactive Student Notebooks. Explain that they will draw two pictures. The top picture will show their family now. The bottom picture will show what their family might look like in the future. They will hide the bottom picture behind two window shutters. Explain that someone looking at their notebook will have to open the shutters to see what their family will be like in the future.

2 **Model the Processing assignment for students, using a transparency of Processing 12.** Draw a picture of your family now and a picture of what your family might look like 10 years in the future. Cut the two window shutters from a copy of *Student Handout 12B: Window to the Future.* Show students how to fold the shutter tabs back and glue them to the sides of the bottom picture. The shutters should fold open and closed.

Student Handout 12B

Window to the Future

Cut out each shutter. Glue them on the picture of your family in the future.

Student Handout 12B

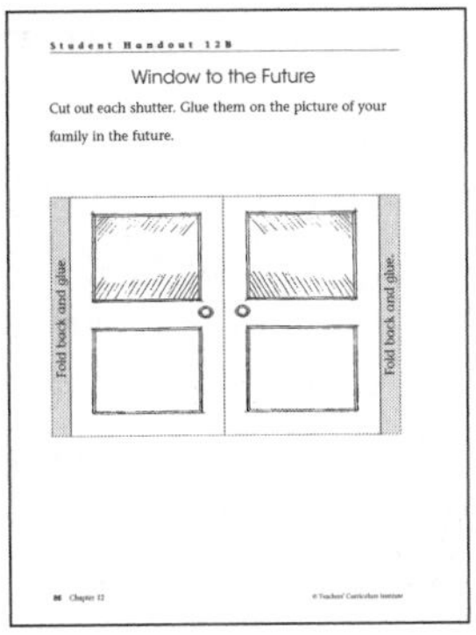

3 **Brainstorm ideas for what students' families might be like in the future.** Ask questions such as these:

- What will you look like? (You might suggest that they draw their families when they themselves are teenagers.)
- What will the other members of your family look like?
- Are there any new family members?
- Where will you live?
- What kind of home will you live in?
- What will your room look like?

4 **Distribute Student Handout 12B and have students complete the Processing assignment.** Students should cut out the shutters on the handout. Tell them to wait until after drawing their pictures in their Interactive Student Notebooks to glue the shutters on the page. Afterward, have students share their completed page with a partner.

Assessment

Masters for the chapter assessment appear in the *Lesson Masters.*
Answers appear below.

Big Ideas

1. match to family with newborn baby
2. match to family moving furniture
3. A

Show You Know

4. The two pictures and their title can serve as a three-point rubric for this item.

English Language Learners

Provide students with vocabulary words so they can annotate the visual elements of this lesson. For example, as they circle the family members on Student Handout 12A, have them write the words *mother, father, grandmother, brother, sister,* and *baby* next to the appropriate people in the image. Similarly, as they complete Reading Further 12 in their Interactive Student Notebooks, help students write words identifying both the old pictures and the modern picture they draw (e.g., *typewriter* and *computer*). After completing the page, have students practice saying the words aloud while pointing to the corresponding pictures.

Students with Special Needs

To assist students with the Processing assignment, give them a written list of the six prompting questions in the Lesson Guide, Processing Step 3. Have them circle two or more of these specific items to illustrate for their future family.

Enrichment

To further personalize the concept that families change over time, ask students to write a simple story about their families through two or three generations: their grandparents, their parents, and themselves. To gather information for their story, they will need to interview older family members about their younger days. Help them come up with interview questions to ask at home. For example: *Where did you live as a child? What was your favorite toy or game? What chores did you have? How was your life different from mine?* Students' stories should emphasize how things have changed over time, comparing their family's past to their present life. Students might include old photos, or pictures they have drawn based on old photos, to illustrate their story.

Enrichment Resources

Have students find out more about how families change over time by exploring the following Enrichment Resources for *Social Studies Alive! My School and Family,* at www.learntci.com.

Internet Connections

These recommended Web sites provide useful and engaging content that enforces skills development and mastery of subjects within the chapter.

Enrichment Readings

These in-depth readings encourage students to explore selected topics related to the chapter. For Chapter 12, you may wish to use one or more of the Enrichment Readings listed in the chapter. You may also find readings that relate the chapter's content directly to your state's curriculum.

Additional Reading Opportunities

These books, which can be read aloud to students, offer opportunities to extend the content in this chapter.

Grandfather's Wrinkles by Kathryn England. Illustrated by Richard McFarland. (New York: Flashlight Press, 2007)

When Lucy asks her grandfather about his wrinkles, he explains that each one came from smiling in joy over a happy family event. As he shares his memories, Lucy learns how family changes affect each family member.

A Kiss Goodbye by Audrey Penn. Illustrated by Barbara L. Gibson. (Terre Haute, IN: Tanglewood Press, 2007)

Chester Raccoon is sad when his family has to move, but he learns that moving to a new home can lead to making new friends.

Love the Baby by Steven L. Layne. Illustrated by Ard Hoyt. (Gretna, LA: Pelican Publishing Co., 2007)

Big brother bunny learns that, despite the apparent drawbacks, a new baby in the family can be a positive change.

Tell Me Again About the Night I Was Born by Jamie Lee Curtis. Illustrated by Laura Cornell. (New York: HarperTrophy, 2000)

This warm and reassuring story explains, in terms that children can understand, how people adopt a baby.

Part A

Think about how life will change when you are older.

1. What new chores will you have? Draw a chore you will do when you are older.

   Answers will vary. Students might show things such as helping to cook,
   helping with laundry, vacuuming, washing the car, or working in the yard or garden.

2. What new things will you be able to do? Draw something you will do when you are older.

   Answers will vary. Students might show things such as staying up later,
   going places by themselves, or learning to drive a car.

Part B

Write two sentences about how Ted's family has changed.

Answers will vary. Possible changes include these: Ted's dad married his first wife and had two children, Meg and Sam; Ted's dad and mom got married; Ted was born; the parents adopted a baby. Look for the use of transition words such as first, next, then, or later in the student's two sentences.

1. _____

_____

_____

2. _____

_____

_____

Families change over time. So do ways of life.

Next to each picture, draw what we use today.

Drawings will vary, but should reflect a modern way to wash clothing. Possible answer: washer or laundromat

Drawings will vary, but should reflect a modern way to create printed words. Possible answer: computer or printer

Drawings will vary, but should reflect a modern way to talk to someone who is not in your presence. Possible answer: cell phone or push-button phone

What Are Family Traditions?

Overview

Students explore their own family traditions and learn about the traditions of others. In the Preview, they consider what they know about how we celebrate three holidays. The Experiential Exercise has students simulate celebrations from two different cultures. In the Reading Further, they learn about some more traditions from around the world and consider whether they have similar traditions in their own families or communities. Then in a Processing assignment, they make a quilt square that shows their family's traditions for celebrating special days.

Objectives

Social Studies

- Name details of traditional holiday celebrations, grouping them in four given categories.
- Compare and contrast one's own family traditions with the traditions of other families.
- Identify a tradition associated with a particular part of the world.
- Create a visual design for a family tradition.

Language Arts

- Listen to acquire knowledge. (speaking and listening)
- Create context-appropriate dialogue for a play. (speaking and listening)

Social Studies Vocabulary

tradition, celebrate, holiday

Materials

Social Studies Alive! My School and Family Big Book and Student Editions

Transparencies 13A–13E

Interactive Student Notebooks

Lesson Masters

- Information Masters 13A–13E
- Student Handouts 13A–13C

mural paper (or bulletin board)

small paper bag

yellow construction paper

ruler

Time Estimates

Preview: 20 min.

Experiential Exercise: 3 sessions (varying lengths)

Reading Further: 25 min.

Processing: 20 min.

Activity	Suggested Time	Materials
Preview • Connecting to Prior Knowledge • Building Background Knowledge • Developing Vocabulary	20 minutes	• *Social Studies Alive! My School and Family* Big Book • Interactive Student Notebooks • Student Handout 13A (1 per student)
Experiential Exercise Experiencing family traditions for birthdays and holidays	*Phase 1* 35 minutes • Roberto's birthday party (Steps 1–8)	• Transparency 13A • Information Master 13A (1 transparency) • Information Masters 13B and 13C • Student Handout 13B (1 copy, cut apart) • small paper bag
	Phase 2 30 minutes • Chinese Lantern Festival (Steps 9–15)	• Transparencies 13B–13D • Interactive Student Notebooks • Information Master 13D (cut out and glued to tag board headband) • Information Master 13E • yellow construction paper, ruler
	Phase 3 20 minutes • Reviewing family traditions (Steps 16 and 17)	• *Social Studies Alive! My School and Family* Big Book and Student Editions, Sections 13.1–13.4 • Interactive Student Notebooks • Information Master 13A (filled in, from Phase 2)
Reading Further Learning about more traditions around the world	25 minutes	• *Social Studies Alive! My School and Family* Big Book and Student Editions, Chapter 13 Reading Further • Transparency 13E • Interactive Student Notebooks
Processing Representing one's own family holiday traditions to make a class quilt	20 minutes	• Interactive Student Notebooks • Student Handout 13C (1 per student, plus 1 transparency) • mural paper (or bulletin board)
Assessment	15 minutes	• Chapter 13 Assessment, Lesson Masters • Chapter 13 Assessment, Digital Teacher Resources

Preview

1 **Connecting to Prior Knowledge:** Help students think about what they already know about celebrating holidays.

- Write "New Year's Day" on the board and read the words aloud. Explain that this is a holiday—a day when many businesses are closed and people do special things. Tell students that the first thing New Year's Day makes you think of is a party hat that you might wear when you stay up until midnight to welcome in the new year. Draw a party hat below the words.

- Have students turn to Preview 13 in their Interactive Student Notebooks. Read the directions and the three holidays named. Ask students to draw the first thing they think for the Fourth of July, Valentine's Day, and Thanksgiving.

- Have students share what they drew for each holiday. Record responses on the board. Ask students what the word *celebrate* means to them. They should understand that the word refers to all the things that we do to make a holiday a special day. Help students recognize that what they have drawn in Preview 13 shows some of the ways people celebrate these holidays.

2 **Building Background Knowledge:** Help students understand the New Idea *tradition*.

- Point out that the things they drew for the Fourth of July, Valentine's Day, and Thanksgiving are all part of our holiday traditions. Traditions are special ways of doing things in a family or in a community.

- Explain that while we see lots of traditions on holidays, traditions can also be part of our daily life. Some of the foods we eat, the clothing we wear, the games we play, and the art we make can all be part of a family or community tradition.

- Turn through the pages of Chapter 13 in the *Social Studies Alive! My School and Family* Big Book to build knowledge about traditions. Encourage students to look carefully at the pictures. On each page, ask: *What tradition do you think this shows? Do you think it is a holiday tradition or a traditional way of life for this family?*

- Prepare students for the quilt project at the end of this lesson. Give each student a copy of *Student Handout 13A: Tradition Survey*. Tell students that this is a letter they will take home to their families, asking how they celebrate special days. Explain that students will use what they learn from their families to make a class quilt of family traditions.

- Over the next few days, remind students of the importance of returning the letter with their family's information. As students turn their letters in, collect them for use in the Processing activity.

3 **Developing Vocabulary:** After discussing the New Ideas—*tradition, celebrate,* and *holiday*—in this Preview, review the terms as they arise in the text.

Student Handout 13A

Experiential Exercise

Phase 1: Acting Out a Latino Family Birthday Party

1 **Prepare materials for Phase 1 of the activity.** Cut the cards from *Student Handout 13B: Birthday Party Assignments.* Count out enough to have one per student, removing some of the duplicate cards for decorations and food as needed to match the number in your class. Place the cards in a paper bag for use in Step 7.

Student Handout 13B

2 **Ask students to tell how they celebrate their birthdays, naming details in four given categories.** Project a transparency of *Information Master 13A: Celebrating Special Days.* As students tell you about the decorations, food, clothing, and activities that are part of their birthday celebrations, record their responses for each category in the first column of the chart. You might include students' names for later reference. Point out that while most families celebrate birthdays, they sometimes celebrate them in different ways.

3 **Project *Transparency 13A: What Are Family Traditions?*** Tell students that they will hear a story about the people pictured on the transparency. Have students make some predictions first. Ask:

- What do you see in the picture?

- What do you think the people are celebrating? What makes you think so?

- What do you think the boy is doing with the stick?

Information Masters 13A and 13B

Explain that this picture shows one family's way of celebrating a birthday. Tell students to listen carefully to the family's story, because they are going to perform a play about this birthday party. Keep the transparency in place as a visual reference.

4 **Read the story on *Information Master 13B: Roberto's Birthday Party.*** Then direct attention to the transparency and ask questions to review the story:

- What are the people celebrating?

- What are some of the decorations?

- What kinds of food are on the table?

- What is the boy with the stick doing?

- What do we call the object that is hanging from a rope?

- What is inside the piñata?

Transparency 13A

5 **Ask students to name details about Roberto's birthday party in the four given categories.** Project Information Master 13A again. As students name the traditional aspects of Roberto's party, record their answers for each category in the second column of the chart.

6 **Have students compare Roberto's birthday party with their own birthday traditions.** In each row of the chart, ask students to find similarities and differences in the birthday celebrations of class members and Roberto's birthday celebration. Keep this transparency on display for reference as students make preparations for the play.

7 **Have students prepare for a play in which they will act out a traditional Latino birthday party.** Bring out the bag you prepared with cards that will identify each student's job.

- Have students draw their assignments from the bag.

- Give drawing paper to those who are preparing props (food and decorations). Encourage them to refer to the chart to recall what special food and decorations Roberto had at his party.

- Meet with the students who are the primary actors. Help them tape their name cards to their clothes so the class will know the roles they are acting out. Explain that you will read the play aloud, and they will pantomime the actions you describe. They will also speak when you prompt them.

- While the rest of the class is preparing the props, rehearse with the actors. Read the play from *Information Master 13C: Play for Roberto's Birthday Party*. Help the actors think of appropriate things to say when it is their turn to speak. If your class knows any Spanish words, encourage actors to include these in their lines.

8 **Prepare the stage and enact the play.** Hang the students' decorations at the front of the room. Arrange desks to resemble a table and set out the food students have drawn.

- Remind the primary actors to be ready for their speaking roles. The rest of the class will act as additional friends at the party.

- Present the play, reading from Information Master 13C.

- Debrief the experience. Ask: *How did you feel as you were doing this activity? What are some things that are the same about Roberto's birthday party and your birthday celebrations? What are some things that are different?*

Reading Strategy: Compare and Contrast

Help students organize their thinking on their own charts. Model labeling a box at the top "Both birthday celebrations" and two columns below "My birthday" and "Roberto's birthday." Students then write similarities and differences in this chart.

Information Master 13C

Phase 2: Acting Out the Dragon Dance for a Chinese Lantern Festival

9 **Prepare materials for Phase 2 of the activity.** Use *Information Master 13D: Dragon Headband* to create one headband for the dragon dance parade. Cut an 8-inch circle from yellow construction paper and tape it firmly to one end of a sturdy ruler.

10 **Use images to introduce the Chinese Lantern Festival.** Let students know that these pictures show a special day that not everyone celebrates.

• Project *Transparency 13B: Chinese Lantern Festival* and ask: *What do you see? What special clothes do you see? What decorations do you see?*

• Project *Transparency 13C: Asian American Family* and ask: *What do you see? What is on the table? What are the people doing?*

• Project *Transparency 13D: Dragon Dance* and ask: *What do you see? What is the animal in the picture? Is it a real animal? How do you think those people make the animal move?*

11 **Read aloud the story on *Information Master 13E: Chinese Lantern Festival*.** Review the information presented in the story by discussing the three transparencies again.

• Project Transparency 13B. Ask: *What holiday are these people celebrating? What are they carrying?* (red lanterns) *What are they wearing?* (red clothing, crowns)

• Project Transparency 13C. Ask: *What are the people doing? What foods do you see?* (roast duck, fruit, rice, tea, rolls)

• Project Transparency 13D. Ask: *What are these people doing? What do they call this part of the parade?* (the dragon dance)

12 **Have students recall details they have learned about the Chinese Lantern Festival.** Project Information Master 13A again and fill in the third column as students answer these questions to identify details in each category:

• How do people decorate their houses for the Lantern Festival?

• What special foods do they eat?

• What kind of clothes do they wear on that day?

• What are the special activities for the day?

13 **Prepare students to act out the traditional Chinese dragon dance.** Project Transparency 13D again as you explain how the students will see what it is like to be part of a dragon dance in the Chinese Lantern Festival.

• Ask students to describe what they remember of the dance from the story. Prompt them with questions such as these, and point out details on the transparency as they are mentioned: *Who walks in front of the dragon?* (a person) *What is this person carrying?* (a red or yellow ball on a stick) *What is the ball supposed to be?* (the sun)

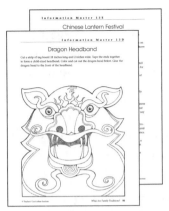

Information Masters 13D and 13E

Transparencies 13B–13D

Speaking and Listening: Prepare to Listen

A lot of new and detailed content is presented orally through the Chinese Lantern Festival story. You can help students focus by using the KWL strategy. Ask students what they already know about this festival (from the images). Then ask what they want to learn about it. Encourage them to listen for the things they want to learn.

- Show students the props you have prepared and explain the activity. To perform a dragon dance, one person will hold up the sun and try to keep it away from the dragon. The rest of the class will form a line, with each person holding onto the shoulders of the person in front. The student at the front of the line acts as the dragon's head and will wear the dragon headband. He or she will lead the line and try to catch the sun.

14 **Have students perform the dragon dance.** You may want to do this outside at recess. Choose one student to carry the sun and another to play the part of the dragon's head. Then have the rest of the students line up to form the dragon's long body. Give a signal for the sun to beginning moving and the dragon to follow it as everyone joins in the dragon dance.

15 **Debrief the experience.** Ask questions such as the following:

- How did you feel when you were doing the dance?

- Was it hard or easy to move as one line?

- Did the line sometimes break? Why did that happen?

Explain that being a dragon dancer requires great skill. People who carry parts of the dragon must be careful to stay together as they move.

Phase 3: Reviewing Family Traditions

16 **Review family traditions by reading Chapter 13.** Read aloud Sections 13.1–13.4 in *Social Studies Alive! My School and Family,* while students follow along in their Student Editions. Ask questions such as the following:

- Section 13.1: *Does your family have any special foods or special clothes? Is there a traditional day or a special time of year when you enjoy these?*

- Section 13.2: *Does your family play any traditional games or tell any traditional stories?*

- Section 13.3: *Does your birthday celebration look anything like the ones in the pictures on this page? What things are the same?*

- Section 13.4: *What other holidays can you name?*

- Summary: *What are traditions?*

17 **Use Reading Notes 13 to review what students have learned about two traditional celebrations.**

- Project the chart on Information Master 13A again and read aloud the information collected in columns 2 and 3.

- Then have students turn to Reading Notes 13 in their Interactive Student Notebooks. Read the directions. Remind students to include pictures of food, clothing, decorations, and special activities for each celebration (Roberto's birthday party and the Chinese Lantern Festival) as they complete the page.

> **Reading Strategy: Make Connections**
>
> Encourage students to make connections between each general statement in the chapter and specific details from the Experiential Exercise. For example, when the text reads "Some families eat special foods," students might remember Robert's tacos, tamales, and Mexican lemonade, or Alice's Chinese dumplings. Ask them to make similar connections for each section of text.

Reading Further: Traditions Around the World

1   **Project *Transparency 13E: Traditions Around the World.*** Ask the following visual discovery questions:

Transparency 13E

• What kind of map is this? *(world map)*

• What sorts of things do you see in the pictures scattered around the map?

• Who can find something that Roberto had at his party?

• Who can find something that was part of the Chinese Lantern Festival?

• Why do you think there are lines connecting each picture to a different place on the world map?

2   **Tell students that this map shows traditions that people have in other parts of the world.**

• Explain that Alice Chang and Roberto Gomez (whose stories they heard) both live in the United States, but their family traditions—the piñata game and the dragon dance—come from other countries. Point out the lines that link the piñata to Mexico and the dragon to China. When people move to the United States from other countries, to join their families or to look for work, they often bring colorful traditions with them. Often, we like the newcomers' traditions and adopt some of them ourselves. At the same time, the newcomers from other countries often adopt some of our traditions as their own.

• Help students locate the United States on the world map. Point out that Mexico is our neighbor to the south, while China is far away and across an ocean.

• Ask students what kind of traditions they think the other pictures are showing. If they are puzzled by some pictures, remind them that they will learn more about these traditions in the story.

3   **Turn to Reading Further 13 in the Big Book.** Read the story aloud while students follow along.

• Point out the little map on each page that shows where in the world this tradition might be found. Pause at the end of each page to have students answer the question, naming any traditions they have or know about that are similar to the one described in the story.

• Help students understand that while some traditions show up in the way people celebrate holidays, other traditions are special ways people have of doing things in everyday life. Have them identify the traditions in this story that are part of everyday life in other countries.

• In your discussion of Veterans Day, tell students that this is not just an American tradition. People in other parts of the world also honor the men and women who fought to keep their countries safe. They give thanks to both heroes who are alive and those who have died. Ask students how they know this picture is from a celebration in our country. *(the U.S. flag)* Also ask how many members of Grace's family are veterans. *(two)* Explain that some families have a tradition of serving in the armed forces.

4 **Have students identify a tradition associated with a particular part of the world where someone might travel.** Ask them to open their Interactive Student Notebooks to Reading Further 13. Read the directions aloud and give an example of one way students might finish the travel poster, such as: *Come to Mexico where the piñata party is a tradition.* Encourage them to use their Student Editions to choose one of the places and traditions mentioned in Reading Further 13.

Processing

1 **Introduce and model the making of individual squares for a class quilt of family traditions.** Explain that each student will make one paper quilt square, showing their family's traditions for celebrating a special day.

- Project a transparency of *Student Handout 13C: Traditions Quilt Square.* Show students how to complete a square by making one of your own.

- Show students where you will hang their finished squares, making a class quilt for wall display.

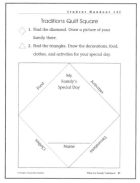

Student Handout 13C

2 **Help students brainstorm special days and related family traditions.** Have them turn to Processing 13 in their Interactive Student Notebooks. Read the directions and explain that they will use this page to brainstorm ideas for their quilt squares.

- Tell students that the special day they use as the subject of their quilt square might be a day that most people celebrate, like a birthday. Or it might be a special day that not everyone celebrates, like the Chinese Lantern Festival.

- Redistribute any surveys (Student Handout 13A) that the students brought back to class. If students like an idea mentioned in their survey from home, they can use that.

- Suggest some other celebrations that students might be familiar with, including holidays such as the Fourth of July, Valentine's Day, and Thanksgiving (from Preview 13); religious events and holidays such as christenings, weddings, first communions, bar mitzvahs and bat mitzvahs, Christmas, Hanukkah, and Ramadan; or cultural holidays such as Kwanzaa, St. Patrick's Day, the Vietnamese New Year (Tet), and the Indian Festival of Lights (Divali).

3 **Have students create a visual design for their chosen family tradition.** Distribute the pattern for the quilt square on Student Handout 13C. Have students use crayons or markers to complete their quilt squares with colorful pictures. Remind them to refer to their brainstorming page as needed.

4   **Put together and hang the class quilt.** Mount the completed squares on white mural paper or a bulletin board. Use a marker to add lines representing stitches. Make the quilt as wide as needed for your class. To help students appreciate the diversity apparent in their class and to encourage respect for one another's traditions, call on students to point out and present their individual squares to their classmates.

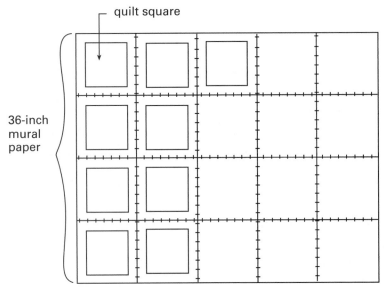

Mark off 9-inch squares with a marker.
Add "stitch" lines.

Assessment

Masters for the chapter assessment appear in the *Lesson Masters*.
Answers appear below.

Big Ideas

1. color yellow: piñata

2. color red: Chinese dragon

3. color brown: drum

Show You Know

4. The bulleted points can serve as a rubric for this item.

English Language Learners

For the play that represents Roberto's birthday party during Phase 1 of the Experiential Exercise, allow students to choose the role with which they feel most comfortable rather than randomly drawing their assignments from the bag. If students are not comfortable performing, let them choose to create props. However, if the students are Spanish-speakers, they may enjoy performing for classmates in their native language. As you work with all students to create the lines of dialogue for the play, allow these students to deliver the lines in Spanish. Then have English-speakers speak the same words in English.

Students with Special Needs

On Reading Notes 13 and Reading Further 13 in their Interactive Student Notebooks, if students have difficulty writing phrases and sentences on their own, have them dictate their ideas to someone who can record the words.

Enrichment

Have students use one of the special family traditions they illustrated for the Processing assignment, or another tradition of their choice, to create a short play like the one they performed for Roberto's birthday party. Have students create props and a few lines of dialogue for one or more characters and then present the play to the class. An additional challenge would be to have students present the skit without identifying the tradition, asking classmates to guess the tradition by using clues from the dialogue, props, and actions.

Enrichment Resources

Have students find out more about different family traditions, here and around the world, by exploring the following Enrichment Resources for *Social Studies Alive! My School and Family,* at www.learntci.com.

Internet Connections

These recommended Web sites provide useful and engaging content that enforces skills development and mastery of subjects within the chapter.

Enrichment Readings

These in-depth readings encourage students to explore selected topics related to the chapter. For Chapter 13, you may wish to use one or more of these Enrichment Readings listed for the chapter. You may also find readings that relate the chapter's content directly to your state's curriculum.

Additional Reading Opportunities

These fiction and nonfiction books, which can be read aloud to students, offer opportunities to extend the content in this chapter.

Chicken Sunday by Patricia Polacco (New York: Scholastic, 1992)

This story about children who find a way to buy an Easter hat for their grandma blends Russian Jewish and African American traditions.

How My Family Lives in America by Susan Kuklin (New York: Simon and Schuster, 1992)

Sanu, Eric, and April are from three American families, but each has a parent who grew up elsewhere: Senegal, Puerto Rico, and Taiwan. One by one, these children explain their family customs, including the stories, arts, and ethnic foods they enjoy. Color photographs accompany their stories.

Juneteenth Jamboree by Carole Boston Weatherford. Illustrated by Yvonne Buchanan. (New York: Lee and Low Books, 2007)

After moving to Texas, Cassie learns what makes June 19 such a special day— it's when African American families celebrate the end of slavery in the United States. Lively illustrations show the foods, dances, parades, balloons, and other traditions related to the holiday.

My First Ramadan by Karen Katz (New York: Holt, 2007)

Through the eyes of a young Muslim boy, readers learn the customs and practices surrounding Ramadan, the ninth month of the Islamic calendar and a time of fasting, feasting, sharing, and prayer.

What Do Good Neighbors Do?

Overview

Students explore their responsibilities as neighbors in a neighborhood. In the Preview, students define their own neighborhood by identifying four places near their home. In a Problem Solving Groupwork activity, groups of four illustrate and assemble puzzles that show examples of actions good neighbors take. In Reading Further, through the retelling of an old tale of barter and exchange, students discover how good neighbors can help satisfy one another's needs and wants. Finally, in the Processing activity, students apply their knowledge by identifying one way they have been a good neighbor.

Objectives

Social Studies

- Define the concepts of neighborhood and neighbors.
- Identify the types of behavior that characterize good neighbors.
- Evaluate behaviors and choose those that illustrate a particular way of being neighborly.
- Analyze the system of barter among neighbors.

Language Arts

- Share ideas and cooperate in making group decisions. (speaking and listening)
- Apply new learning in a personal statement. (writing)

Social Studies Vocabulary

neighbor, next door, neighborhood

Materials

Social Studies Alive! My School and Family Big Book and Student Editions

Transparencies 14A and 14B

Interactive Student Notebooks

Lesson Masters

- Information Masters 14A and 14B
- Student Handouts 14A–14D

Interactive Desk Maps

construction paper

chart paper

Time Estimates

Preview: 20 min.

Problem Solving Groupwork: 2 sessions (25 min. and 35 min.)

Reading Further: 30 min.

Processing: 20 min.

Activity	Suggested Time	Materials
Preview • Connecting to Prior Knowledge • Building Background Knowledge • Developing Vocabulary	20 minutes	• Interactive Student Notebooks • Interactive Desk Maps
Problem Solving Groupwork Exploring the behaviors that characterize good neighbors	25-minute session • Identifying actions that a good neighbor takes (Steps 1–3) 35-minute session • Making a poster (Steps 4–9)	• *Social Studies Alive! My School and Family,* Student Editions and Big Book, Sections 14.1–14.4 • Transparency 14A • Interactive Student Notebooks • Information Master 14A (2 copies, with one cut apart as a model) • Information Master 14B (1 transparency) • Student Handouts 14A–14C (enough copies to give each group of 4 a two-page puzzle) • chart paper • construction paper, 12 by 18 inches (1 sheet per group of 4)
Reading Further Reading an old tale about neighbors who barter	30 minutes	• *Social Studies Alive! My School and Family,* Student Editions, Chapter 14 Reading Further • Transparency 14B • Interactive Student Notebooks • Student Handout 14D (one copy for each small group)
Processing Creating Good Neighbor awards	20 minutes	• Interactive Student Notebooks
Assessment	15 minutes	• Chapter 14 Assessment, Lesson Masters • Chapter 14 Assessment, Digital Teacher Resources

Preview

1 Connecting to Prior Knowledge: Help students identify the places and buildings that make up their own neighborhood.

- Have students turn to Preview 14 in their Interactive Student Notebooks. Read the directions aloud. Then have students complete the page, drawing their homes and four places nearby. Explain that students may draw houses, apartment buildings, stores, parks, playgrounds, firehouses, the school—any buildings or places they can walk to from their homes.

- Call on volunteers to share the places they drew. Explain that all these places are part of their neighborhood. Ask if any of the places they drew are next door to their home. Establish that *next door* means the very next house or apartment you come to when you leave your door.

2 Building Background Knowledge: Help students define *neighbors* as the people who live and work in a neighborhood.

- Distribute an Interactive Desk Map to each pair of students, turned to the side that shows a neighborhood map. Ask: *What does this map show?* (streets and places in a neighborhood) *What buildings and places can you name in this neighborhood?* (houses, apartment building, school, grocery store, baseball field, playground)

- Help students read the street names on the map. Then ask them to think about the people who might live in this neighborhood. Divide students into small groups. Assign each group one specific location on the map, and ask them to make up the names of at least three people who might live, work, or play in that location.

- Have groups share with the class the names of the people they made up, point out on the map where in the neighborhood you would find them, and tell what these people do in the neighborhood—that is, do they live there or work there? What kind of work do they do?

- Next, write on the board: *Neighbors are people who* . . . Ask students to suggest ways to finish the sentence. In addition to any other ideas they have, students should establish that neighbors are all the people who live and work in a particular neighborhood.

3 Developing Vocabulary: After discussing the New Ideas—*neighbor, next door,* and *neighborhood*—in this Preview, reinforce them as they arise in the text.

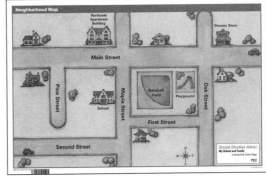

Interactive Desk Map

> **Reading Strategy:
> Use Phonetic Clues**
>
> Write the words *neighbor* and *neighborhood* on the board. Draw lines to break the words into syllables:
> neigh | bor
> neigh | bor | hood
> Ask students to identify the letter and sound they hear at the beginning of each syllable. Have the whole class repeat the words, clapping once for each syllable as you point to it.

Problem Solving Groupwork

1 Help students identify the types of behavior that characterize a good neighbor.

- Using the *Social Studies Alive: My School and Family* Big Book, read aloud the section titles in Chapter 14. On each page, ask students how the picture is connected to the section title.

- Draw this three-column chart on chart paper (to save for continued use):

Good Neighbors

Help Each Other	Get Along	Take Care of Their Neighborhood

- Read Chapter 14 in the Big Book as students follow along in their Student Editions. After reading Section 14.1, ask students: *Who are some of the neighbors who live and work in your neighborhood?*

- Pause after reading each of the next three sections to generate a list of actions students have taken or can think of taking to help their neighbors, get along with their neighbors, and take care of their neighborhood. Write or draw their responses under the appropriate headings in the chart.

2 Ask students to identify further examples of being a good neighbor. Project *Transparency 14A: What Do Good Neighbors Do?* Ask students to point to any images that show neighbors

- helping each other. *(two women helping each other fix a fence, a girl helping a boy rollerblade)*

- getting along. *(adults working together, children playing together)*

- taking care of their neighborhood. *(picking up toys, fixing the fence, gardening, mowing the lawn, decorating a porch)*

Add these actions to the appropriate categories in the chart. Keep the chart for review before students make their posters.

3 Have students complete Reading Notes 14 to describe how they can be good neighbors. Ask them to turn to Reading Notes 14 in their Interactive Student Notebooks. Read the directions aloud. Then, as a class, read aloud all ten sentences that describe ways we might behave as neighbors, good or not so good. Have students circle only those sentences that describe good neighbors.

Vocabulary Development: Recognize Action Words

Reread Sections 14.1–14.4 in the Big Book, asking students to name the verb or verb phrase in each sentence that describes what the neighbors do. Make a list of these action words and tell students we call these words *verbs*. Ask students to think of other verbs to add to the list.

Transparency 14A

4 **Outside of class, prepare a model for the work to be done on a Good Neighbors poster.** Cut the puzzle pieces from one copy of *Information Master 14A: Sample Puzzle.*

5 **To introduce the poster activity, review with students the ways good neighbors act.**

- Call attention to the chart you created earlier. Ask students to read the actions in each category with you. Ask them if they have any other ideas to add to the chart.

- Tell students they will work in groups of four to make posters that show how good neighbors act. They will make their posters by illustrating and assembling puzzle pieces.

6 **Model the Good Neighbors poster activity.** Choose three children to work with you as a small group of four in front of the class. Follow these steps:

- Show the class both pages of uncut Student Handout 14A. Point out that each page has two puzzle pieces. Let students know that they will first cut each page in half, so that each person in the group has one puzzle piece. Then each student will cut out his or her own puzzle piece. Explain that you have already done the cutting for your group to save time.

- Give yourself and each student in your group one puzzle piece from Student Handout 14A. Demonstrate how to assemble the puzzle. Point out that each puzzle piece has a star at the top so students always know which way the piece should go in the puzzle.

- Explain that when the puzzle is put together, it makes a sentence. The sentence will tell students what kind of pictures they will need to draw. Read the sentence on the sample puzzle: "We Help Keep Our Neighbors Safe." This means the group must draw pictures showing things that people do to help keep their neighbors safe. Emphasize that they will not glue the puzzle pieces down yet.

- After reading the sentence, your group should discuss four ideas to illustrate it. For example, they might draw someone riding her bike carefully, picking up toys on the sidewalk, helping a younger child cross the street, or walking a dog on a leash.

- Be certain students understand that they must draw only things that illustrate the sentence on their puzzle. To check their understanding, ask if a picture of a boy mowing a lawn would illustrate "We Help Keep Our Neighbors Safe." *(no)*

- After students have chosen four ways to illustrate the sentence, each person in the group will draw, color, and label one picture on his or her puzzle piece. Explain that no one should begin drawing until everyone in the group knows what to draw.

- Once students complete their illustrations and labels, they will arrange and glue their four puzzle pieces on a sheet of construction paper.

Information Master 14A

7 **Project a transparency of *Information Master 14B: Roles for Your Group.***
Read aloud the four roles. Divide the class into mixed-ability groups of four,
and assign each student a role in the group.

8 **Have each group evaluate kinds of neighborly behavior.** Their goal is
to choose four actions that will best illustrate the sentence on their Good
Neighbor poster.

- Give each group a sheet of construction paper and a two-page puzzle copied
from *Student Handouts 14A–14C: Puzzles A–C.*

- Have groups follow the steps you modeled to create their posters. Remind
them of their individual roles. Emphasize that all four students must cut out
their own puzzle pieces neatly along the dashed lines.

- Point out that an important part of the puzzle is deciding, as a group, what
pictures best illustrate their puzzle sentence. If students need ideas for these
pictures, encourage groups to refer to the class chart.

- Emphasize that the pictures on all four pieces must be finished before the
group glues any piece down. (**Note:** You may want to check each group's
assembled puzzle before allowing students to glue it.)

9 **Allow time for groups to share their posters with the class.** Have each
Presenter show the group's poster, explaining the pictures they drew and how
the pictures reflect the message on the puzzle.

Reading Further: The Apple Dumpling

1 **Project *Transparency 14B: The Apple Dumpling* and tell students that it
illustrates the story you are about to read.** Ask questions such as these to
help students make some predictions about the story:

- What do you see in this picture?

- Does this woman seem to have any next-door neighbors?

- Do you think this story is real or make-believe? What makes you think so?

- This story is about a woman who wants some apples, but we see her picking
plums. What do you think she is going to do?

2 **Turn to Reading Further 14 in the Big Book and read the title.**

- Ask: *Who knows what an apple dumpling is?* (an apple sprinkled with spices,
wrapped in dough, and baked in the oven)

- Point out that the story begins with the words "Once upon a time." Ask:
When you hear those words, what do you know about the story? (It's a make-
believe story, like a fairy tale or folktale; it takes place long ago.)

- Read aloud the tale in the Big Book while students follow along in their
Student Editions. (**Note:** This is a retelling of a story by the same name in *The
Story-Teller* by Maud Lindsay, published by Lothrop, Lee, and Shepard, 1915.)

Information Master 14B

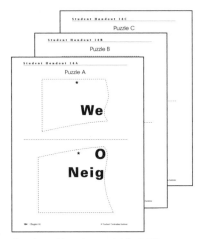
Student Handouts 14A–14C

Transparency 14B

3 **Have students retell the story in sequence and discuss how the neighbors helped one another with their trades.**

- Distribute a copy of *Student Handout 14D: Story Cards* to each small group. Have students cut the three handout pages in half to make six story cards.

- Ask students to work together in their small groups to put the six story cards in order.

- Display the extra set of Story Cards in random order. You might use the chalk tray, a bulletin board, or chart paper and removable tape. Call on students from different groups to come up one at a time and help put the cards in sequence.

- Have students retell the story in their own words, using the posted story cards as prompts. Be sure that students describe each trade the woman made. Explain that making trades like these, where no money is involved, is also called *bartering*. Bartering works only if two people can agree that each person wants what the other one has and they are each happy to make the trade.

- For each transaction in the story, have students identify why the neighbor wanted to trade and why the apple dumpling woman was willing to trade even when she couldn't get the apples she wanted. Refer students to specific paragraphs if they need help remembering the woman's reasoning.

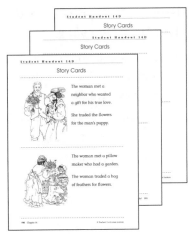

Student Handout 14D

4 **Help students compare the process of bartering with the process of trading for money.** Ask questions such as the following:

- If your family wanted some apples, how would you get them? (*find an apple tree, buy them at the store*)

- If you want to buy something, what do you need to have to trade? (*money*)

- What is one way for people to get the money they need to buy things? (*working at a job, selling something*)

- Which do you think makes it easier to get what you want: bartering or trading for money? What makes you think so? (*Students should recognize that the woman had to make four trades to get apples, whereas it takes just one trade to buy something with money.*)

- Have you ever traded with a friend or neighbor, at home or at school, to get something you wanted? Who traded with you? What did you trade? Were both of you happy with the trade?

- Have you ever traded money to get something you wanted? What was it?

- Would you rather trade for money or barter to get things you want? Why?

5 Have students propose further neighborly actions for the characters in *The Apple Dumpling*.

- Tell students to turn to Reading Further 14 in their Interactive Student Notebooks. Read the directions aloud. Then ask students to describe in their own words the two problems pictured.

- Help students brainstorm ways that one or more of the neighbors could help solve each problem. As words come up in discussion, create a Word Bank that students can use in writing their sentences.

Processing

1 Help students recall their own experiences with being good neighbors. Call attention to the Good Neighbors posters that students created in groups and review the three categories of what good neighbors do: *help each other, get along,* and *take care of their neighborhood.* Then ask students to think of specific things they have done to be good neighbors.

2 Have students create awards to celebrate their neighborliness. Ask students to turn to Processing 14 in their Interactive Student Notebooks.

- Tell students that they will create a Good Neighbor award for themselves, honoring something they have done to be a good neighbor.

- Point out that they will draw a picture of what they did at the top of the award. On the lines, they will write a sentence explaining their picture.

- Invite volunteers to show their awards to the class, explaining why they see themselves as good neighbors.

Assessment

Masters for the chapter assessment appear in the *Lesson Masters*. Answers appear below.

Big Ideas

1. (mowing a lawn) We take care of our neighborhood.
2. (picking up toys on sidewalk) We help keep our neighbors safe.
3. (playing together) We get along with our neighbors.
4. B

Show You Know

5. The bulleted points can serve as a rubric for this item.

English Language Learners

For the Processing assignment, allow students to dictate the sentence describing their deed as a good neighbor. Then transcribe their sentence for them or write it out for them to copy or trace.

Students with Special Needs

Include special needs students in the group that works with you to model creating the Good Neighbors poster. This will give them a chance to practice the activity before working with their peers, allow them to experience success from the beginning of the activity, and enable them to assist group members once they begin the Problem Solving Groupwork activity.

Enrichment

Have students create their own barter story with themselves as the main character, using *The Apple Dumpling* as a model. As a prewriting activity, have each of them identify something they want or need, something they have to offer in a trade, and four things their friends might want to trade. Then have each student create a series of four pictures that show the sequence of exchanges they make and with whom, captioning each picture with one or two sentences. They can share their picture stories with their classmates.

Enrichment Resources

Have students find out more about neighbors and neighborhoods by exploring the following Enrichment Resources for *Social Studies Alive! My School and Family,* at www.learntci.com.

Internet Connections

These recommended Web sites provide useful and engaging content that enforces skills development and mastery of subjects within the chapter.

Enrichment Readings

These in-depth readings encourage students to explore selected topics related to the chapter. For Chapter 14, you may wish to use one or more of the Enrichment Readings listed for the chapter. You may also find readings that relate the chapter's content directly to your state's curriculum.

Additional Reading Opportunities

The following fiction and nonfiction books, which can be read aloud to students, offer opportunities to extend the content in this chapter.

And to Think That We Thought That We'd Never Be Friends by Mary Ann Hoberman. Illustrated by Kevin Hawkes. (New York: Dragonfly Books, 2003)

Noisy new neighbors head off a neighborhood argument by asking everyone to join their band. Soon the entire neighborhood joins in the fun. This clever tale told in rhyme teaches positive ways to deal with conflict.

Be My Neighbor by Maya Ajmera and John D. Ivanko (Watertown, MA: Charlesbridge Publishing, 2004)

Through captivating photographs, this book from A Global Fund for Children explores the concept of community and characteristics of a neighborhood around the world—including the responsibility to improve one's neighborhood and the lives of those who live there.

Cool Ali by Nancy Poydar (New York: Margaret K. McElderry, 1996)

As neighbors fuss about the summer heat outside a city apartment building, Ali uses colored chalk to surround these people with "cool" scenes of lakes, snowstorms, and polar bears—her way of being a good neighbor.

Circle sentences that describe a good neighbor.

(We say hello to our neighbors.)

(We keep our yard clean.)

(We walk our dog on a leash.)

(We pick up trash
in our neighborhood.)

We pick our neighbors' flowers
without permission.

We let our dog run in our

neighbor's yard.

We wave to our neighbors.

We water our neighbors' plants

when they go away.

We feed our neighbors' pets

when they go away.

We drop trash on the street.

	1	2	3	4	5	6	7	8	9	10	11	12	13	14
Map and Globe Skills														
Recognize maps and globes as models						•							•	
Use map tools						•								
Directions/compass rose						•								
Symbols						•								
Identify locations				•		•							•	
Relative (spatial relationships, orientation)						•								
Use different types of maps				•		•							•	
Political maps				•		•							•	
Citizenship and Participation Skills														
Respect American heritage			•	•	•			•					•	
Recognize rights and responsibilities of citizenship	•		•	•	•						•			•
Participate in groups	•		•		•	•	•	•		•				•
Respect points of view	•	•			•	•								•
Assume leader and follower roles					•					•				•
Resolve conflicts	•		•		•									
Graphic and Visual Skills														
Interpret graphic information		•	•	•			•	•			•			•
Graphs								•			•			
Charts		•	•	•			•							•
Timelines							•							
Analyze photographs and other images	•	•	•	•	•	•	•	•	•	•	•	•	•	•

	1	2	3	4	5	6	7	8	9	10	11	12	13	14
Critical Thinking Skills														
Classify		•					•	•	•	•	•		•	
Compare and contrast		•	•		•	•	•		•			•	•	
Sequence							•			•		•		•
Cause and effect	•		•				•							•
Analyze		•	•	•						•		•	•	•
Evaluate		•												•
Draw conclusions	•	•	•	•	•	•			•	•		•	•	
Make inferences	•	•	•	•			•		•			•		•
Generalize	•	•		•	•	•			•	•	•		•	•
Predict	•		•		•		•					•		
Make decisions			•											•
Solve problems	•				•					•				•
Identify point of view							•	•		•		•		
Analyze primary sources				•	•		•		•			•		
Support a position	•		•							•	•			
Reading/Language Arts and Study Skills														
Apply social studies content reading skills	•	•	•	•	•	•	•	•	•	•	•	•	•	•
Use expository text features	•	•	•	•	•	•	•	•	•	•	•	•	•	•
Identify main idea and details				•				•		•				•
Summarize		•		•			•		•					
Ask and answer questions	•	•	•	•	•	•	•	•	•	•	•	•	•	•
Develop vocabulary	•	•	•	•	•	•	•	•	•	•	•	•	•	•
Write for a variety of social studies purposes	•	•	•	•	•	•	•	•	•	•	•	•	•	•
Listen to acquire information	•	•		•	•	•					•	•	•	
Use speaking skills to communicate effectively	•	•	•	•	•	•	•	•	•	•	•	•	•	•
Conduct research				•			•							

Lesson Guide

Photographs

Front Cover
Ableimages/Getty Images

Title Page
Ableimages/Getty Images

Chapter 3
41: Courtesy of the City of Bell-flower, CA

Chapter 4
55 T: RF/Getty Images 55 CT: Michael Malyszko/Getty Images 55 CB: Patti McConville/Getty Images 55 B: Bruce Ayres/Getty Images

Chapter 12
158 T: Culver Pictures, Inc./SuperStock 158 C: RF/Corbis 158 B: Petrified Collection-The Image Bank/Getty Images

Art

Chapter 1
10 L: Doug Roy 10-11: DJ Simison

Chapter 2
24: Jon Goodell 25: Jon Goodell

Chapter 3
37: Susan Jaekel 38: Susan Jaekel 39: Susan Jaekel 40: Susan Jaekel

Chapter 4
56: Gary Undercuffler

Chapter 8
111: Carol Newsome

Chapter 9
122: Jane McCreary 123: Jane McCreary 124: Jane McCreary

Chapter 12
157: DJ Simison

Chapter 14
180: Len Ebert 181: Len Ebert

Placards

Photographs

Front Cover
Ableimages/Getty Images

Chapter 8
9: ©2002 Stephen Simpson-FPG/Getty Images 10: ©2002 Stephanie Rausser-FPG/Getty Images 11: ©2002 AJA Productions-The Image Bank/Getty Images 12: ©2002 Arthur Tilley-FPG/Getty Images 13: ©2002 Romilly Lockyer-The Image Bank/Getty Images 14: ©2002 Jeff Smith-The Image Bank/Getty Images 15: ©2002 Michel Gounot-FPG/Getty Images 16: Corbis 17: ©2002 Jerry Kobalenko-Stone/Getty Images 18: ©2002 Angelo Cavalli-The Image Bank/Getty Images 19: RF/Getty Images 20: Eye Wire/Getty Images

Chapter 10
21-23: K-PHOTOS/Alamy 24-26: RF-American Highlights/Digital Vision 27-29: Diane Macdonald/Getty Images

Chapter 11
30: Michele Westmorland/Getty Images 31: Ryan McVay/Getty Images 32: Steve Mason/Getty Images 33: Stephen Simpson/Getty Images 34: RF/Getty Images 35: Barbara Peacock/Getty Images

Art

Chapter 1
1: Renate Lohmann 2: Renate Lohmann 3: Renate Lohmann 4: Renate Lohmann 5: Renate Lohmann 6: Renate Lohmann 7: Renate Lohmann 8: Renate Lohmann

Artists represented by Ann Remen-Willis, Artist Representative and Art Manager:

Len Ebert
Jon Goodell
Susan Jaekel
Renate Lohmann
Jane McCreary
Carol Newsome
Doug Roy
DJ Simison
Gary Undercuffler